THE LITTLE BOOK OF
FORENSICS

50 of the world's most infamous criminal cases solved by science

D0029432

DAVID OWEN

THE LITTLE BOOK OF
FORENSICS

50 of the world's most infamous criminal cases solved by science

DAVID OWEN

Collins

An Imprint of HarperCollinsPublishers

Contents

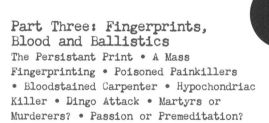

Introduction

Forensic science remains a fascinating subject for many people outside the crime fighting services. The ingenuity and sophistication of the techniques used and the information they can reveal about a crime, have all the appeal of a whodunit by masters of detective fiction like Agatha Christie, P. D. James, or Sir Arthur Conan Doyle. The subject is even of increasing interest to criminals themselves, who are becoming aware of the extra precautions they need to take when planning to commit a crime, to eliminate the danger of being caught and convicted as a consequence of the evidence they might leave behind.

The development of forensic science has allowed advances in a wide range of different fields. By studying stab or impact wounds on a victim's body, investigators can discover a profusion of hidden clues and information: the type of weapon used, the position of the attacker at the moment the wounds were inflicted, whether he or she was right-handed or left-handed, even the height and physical strength of the attacker. Ballistics evidence can reveal whether a particular gun was used to kill or wound a victim, while finger-printing can prove who held the gun at the fatal moment, and trace evidence can determine how close the gun was to the victim when the shots were fired.

Blood evidence can be particularly crucial in revealing a whole range of facts about a violent attack. The spatter pattern of blood  drops on the floor or walls of a crime scene can show the movements of both attacker and victim at the time. By studying the blood flow from individual wounds, forensic experts can determine whether particular blows were struck when the victim was alive or already dead. Ever since blood groups were first isolated, a combination of

different markers in blood samples can be
used to narrow down the identification of
an otherwise anonymous victim, or to
reject individuals from a list of potential
suspects. More recently, the final link in
the chain has been the ability to establish
the identities of victims and criminals alike
using powerful techniques for retrieving and
analyzing DNA evidence from the tiniest
conceivable amounts of material and this has
provided one of the most powerful weapons in
the forensic armory.

Most recent developments reflect an increasing
effort to obtain evidence for identifying and convicting terrorists,
which often involves different electronic methods such as images
from CCTV cameras or even remotely piloted aircraft, mobile
phone records (including accurate positional information relating
to calls and timings) and e-mail messages. This adds up to a vital
new area of forensic science, largely preserved from public scrutiny
because of the demands of secrecy and security.

As forensic science becomes more capable, it demands greater
care in the collecting and preserving of evidence: the more sensitive
the technique, the greater the danger of contamination which could
render the evidence unreliable or even misleading. The examples
outlined in this book show how the growing power and reliability
of forensic science has been used to convict a wide range of
criminals in every kind of crime. One prediction can be made with
confidence – that forensic science will continue to advance and
become an even more formidable enemy of the criminal, the spy,
the terrorist, and the killer in the future than it has in the past.

Part One:
Cause of Death

Death Dealing Doctor

Where:	New York, USA
When:	January–March 1916
Culprit:	Dr. Arthur Waite
Victims:	Mr. and Mrs. John Peck
Cause of death:	germs and poison
Forensic technique:	toxicology

The Crime

When the body of a possible murder victim is given a post-mortem to determine the cause of death, one of the first signs examiners look for is the presence of any known poisons. But what happens when the lethal ingredients that led to the victim's demise are not chemical poisons, but germs spread by diseases, some of which can prove fatal through natural misfortune rather than murderous intent? If a murderer could harness these germs and bacteria as an effective murder weapon, how could investigators possibly determine whether a victim had died from natural causes or purposefully been exposed to the deadly germs by a human assailant?

This was the line of thought that influenced Dr. Arthur Warren Waite, a dentist in New York who shared his luxury apartment on Riverside Drive with his wife's retired parents. His father-in-law, John Peck, had built up a sizeable fortune after a career as a pharmacist in the Middle West, and Waite longed to inherit as much of the money as possible. The problem was that neither parent seemed in poor health, but it occurred to Waite that it might be possible to give nature a helping hand, by causing Peck to ingest harmful bacteria which would trigger an entirely convincing onset of a serious disease, followed by a severe physical decline and ultimate death, without anyone being held responsible.

The Case

Waite began by setting his sights on John Peck's wife. He carefully isolated a mixture of diphtheria and influenza germs, and added these to her food. After a series of doses, the elderly woman became ill, and her condition steadily

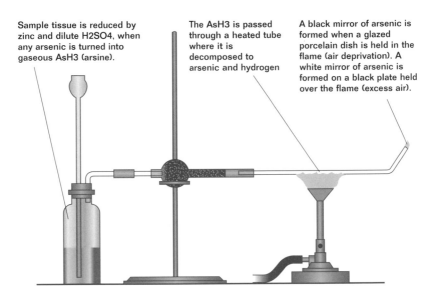

Sample tissue is reduced by zinc and dilute H2SO4, when any arsenic is turned into gaseous AsH3 (arsine).

The AsH3 is passed through a heated tube where it is decomposed to arsenic and hydrogen

A black mirror of arsenic is formed when a glazed porcelain dish is held in the flame (air deprivation). A white mirror of arsenic is formed on a black plate held over the flame (excess air).

Above Demonstration of Marsh's test for arsenic, developed in the 1820s, before which the odorless poison was untraceable in the human body.

deteriorated, until she finally died in January 1916. Waite then shifted his efforts to her husband, but his method did not work so effectively on his second target. It seemed John Peck's constitution was disconcertingly immune to a whole range of nasty bugs, and every weapon in Waite's locker was proving ineffective.

First he tried the diphtheria mixture, with no results. Then he prescribed a nasal spray to aid his victim's breathing, which he had contaminated with tuberculosis germs, but even this failed to produce the planned result. He tried influenza and typhoid, but still the old man remained obstinately healthy. Finally, Waite's impatience overcame all the care and caution he had taken so far in his efforts. Determined to hasten his father-in-law's death, he added a dose of what he described to their family servant simply as "medicine" to tea and soup served to Peck one evening. The "medicine" did exactly what he hoped it would do. A man who appeared to the family doctor as healthy only the day before died on March 12, 1916, just two months after his late wife.

The Evidence

The medicine administered to the unfortunate John Peck was nothing less than a lethal dose of arsenic. Unluckily for the devious dentist, there was a reliable test for the presence of this poison which had been developed by James Marsh, a London chemist, in the 1820s, and this was well known to the investigators. The first step of the test is to place tissue samples from the victim, together with any stomach contents, on to a zinc plate. Then sulphuric acid is poured on to the plate, and in the ensuing reaction any arsenic present in either tissue or stomach contents absorbs the hydrogen from the acid and is given off as a gas. This is collected and passed down a heated tube and then allowed to cool, where the mixture forms white crystals of arsenious oxide. When samples were taken from John Peck's body, the crystals showed exactly what Dr. Warren Waite had turned to in his haste to be rid of his father-in-law.

The Outcome

With evidence as clear as this, the trial was something of a formality. Dr. Arthur Warren Waite was convicted of John Peck's murder, and before his execution he admitted the ingenious and successful methods he had used for poisoning his mother-in-law without incurring any suspicion at all. Had he persevered with these ideas, in time Mr. Peck may have suffered the same fate as his wife without anyone being the wiser.

The Hanging That Never Was

Where: Crowborough, UK
When: December 5, 1924
Culprit: Norman Thorne
Victim: Elsie Cameron
Cause of death: beaten to death
Forensic technique: pathology

The Crime

A common mistake made by murderers is to try to disguise their crime by implying that their victim committed suicide. In most cases, expert forensic investigators are able to isolate factors which prove that an individual did not take his or her own life, but was the victim of murder. One such case was that of Elsie Cameron, a London typist who was involved with a struggling Sussex poultry farmer called Norman Thorne. He lived in a run-down shack at Crowborough, where the couple would spend occasional nights together before she traveled back to work the next day. Elsie desperately wanted to marry, but Thorne refused. Matters came to a head in November 1924, when Elsie wrote to Thorne claiming she was pregnant. She said she would come down to see him on December 5 when he could finally do his duty and make arrangements for their wedding. Five days later, her father reported her missing.

The Case

Police interviewed Thorne, who gave every sign of genuine concern for the missing girl, but insisted she had never arrived as expected. Later two witnesses said they had recognized Elsie making her way to the farm on the evening of December 5, a story confirmed by another local resident returning from holiday. Police interviewed Thorne again, and started searching the farm, where they found Elsie's overnight bag.

Thorne changed his story; he admitted that she had arrived at the farm, that they had then argued in his shack and he had stormed out, refusing to discuss their impending wedding. When he returned, he was appalled to find she had hanged herself from the main roof beam. He admitted to a fit of blind panic, in which he had cut down the corpse, dismembered it, and buried the fragments in the chicken enclosure.

Elsie's body parts were dug up and a post-mortem was carried out to verify the cause of death. The famous criminal pathologist, Sir Bernard Spilsbury, began by examining her neck very closely for signs of bruising from the rope, which would have applied lethal pressure to the blood vessels leading to the brain. Although there was no sign of any of the expected damage, there were bruises in plenty, all over her face, head, and limbs. The conclusion was simple, and fatal for Thorne's explanation of events. She had not died by hanging at all, but had clearly been beaten to death. Thorne was arrested and charged with Elsie's murder.

The Evidence

The defense team set out to discredit Spilsbury's evidence as vigorously as they could. They retained the services of another eminent pathologist, Dr. Robert Bronte, who was a bitter rival of Spilsbury, and welcomed the chance to refute his findings. After carrying out a second post-mortem, he claimed that he had indeed found marks on her neck which could have resulted from a suicidal hanging. Spilsbury insisted that these were merely natural creases in the skin of the victim's neck. Bronte refuted this, maintaining that the marks on her neck were consistent with signs of bruising, but Spilsbury stood his ground, and the evidence appeared in danger of deadlock.

The Outcome

What finally decided the case was a closer examination of the beam from which Thorne had supposedly found the girl's body hanging. If a rope had indeed been tied around the beam and then subjected to the shock of a body falling, there would almost certainly have been detectable grooving caused by the rope being pulled tight. Even more significantly, there was a thick layer of dust on the upper surface of the beam where a casual observer would not have looked. At the very least a rope tied around the beam should have disturbed the dust, but the thick layer showed no marks at all. The evidence proved damning, and fatal for the poultry farmer. He was found guilty, and hanged for the murder of Elsie Cameron on April 22, 1925.

Aunt Thallie's Deadly Cup of Tea

Where:	Sydney, Australia
When:	1947
Culprit:	Caroline Grills
Victims:	several family members
Cause of death:	thallium poisoning
Forensic technique:	toxicology

The Crime

On the face of it, the death of 87-year-old Christina Mickelson in Sydney, Australia in 1947 was hardly suspicious at all. When her friend Angeline Thomas died soon afterward, there seemed no cause for concern, as she too was in her 80s. However, the following year a younger relative, 60-year-old John Lundberg fell seriously ill. His hair fell out, he became progressively weaker, and he was dead within weeks. By now the members of the Mickelson family were becoming seriously worried, and when Mary Ann Mickelson also fell ill and died with similar symptoms to Lundberg, their fears intensified.

The Case

Police looked for a common factor to link these deaths. They found one in a family member who had helped nurse all the family members before they died. Caroline Grills was 63 years old and had married Christina Mickelson's stepson, Richard Grills, 40 years earlier, and they had four sons and a daughter. Now a grandmother and valued member of the extended family, her dumpy figure and thick-framed spectacles appeared regularly in their homes, bringing homemade cakes and cookies, and making endless cups of tea for her invalid charges. Though reluctant to cast suspicion on their "Aunt Carrie," the family could not help noticing that whenever she failed to visit, the sickness would recede, only to reappear when she was back on duty.

Below The Reinsch test is used to detect the presence of one or more heavy metals in a biological sample. The appearance of a silvery coating on the copper may indicate Mercury. A dark coating indicates the presence of another metal, such as thallium.

Copper strip inserted into a hydrochloric acid solution and dissolved suspect body fluid or tissue

A dark coating indicative of the presence of one of the metals, such as thallium

The Evidence

At last the situation reached a crisis point. John Lundberg's widow Eveline, and their daughter Christine Downey, began to suffer from symptoms similar to those of their recently deceased relatives—extreme fatigue, difficulty in speaking and moving, loss of hair, and progressive blindness. One family member was worried enough to contact the police. The symptoms suggested a case of thallium poisoning, so a cup of tea, made for one of the victims, was analyzed using the Reinsch test, a method used to detect the presence of certain heavy metals. The test sample is added to a solution of hydrochloric acid, and a copper strip is then added to the mixture. The presence of heavy metal contaminants is revealed by deposits of the metal in question on the strip, and further tests can then reveal whether this is arsenic, antimony, or thallium, all of which are poisonous.

The results were clear. The tea was indeed laced with thallium, and even though Caroline Grills was arrested so that the imminent danger to the victims was removed, Eveline Lundberg was to lose her eyesight because of the poison. Police also took out an exhumation order to test the bodies of two of her earlier suspected victims, and both turned out to contain large enough quantities of thallium to confirm they too had been poisoned. In fact, the case took place in the context of a minor epidemic of thallium poisoning; five other women in Sydney had also been charged with poisoning members of their families. Thallium was a popular poison, as it was the basis of a rat poison released on the market to combat a rat infestation in the city. It was colorless, odorless, and tasteless, making it difficult for victims to realize there was anything sinister in what they were eating or drinking.

The Outcome

Caroline Grills was arrested and charged with the attempted murders of Eveline Lundberg and Christine Downey on May 11, 1953. These were the cases where the evidence was strongest since these were the victims for whom Grills had made the tea that had tested positive for thallium. She claimed her relatives had given evidence against her because of police pressure, but she was found guilty and sentenced to death on October 15, 1953. Six months later her appeal was turned down and her sentence was commuted to life imprisonment, but she only served six and a half years before she contracted peritonitis and died in hospital on October 6, 1960. Her motives for killing members of her family remained a mystery to the end. During her time in prison she proved extremely popular with other inmates, who renamed her "Aunt Thally."

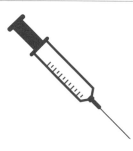

Clues in Blood

Where:	Bradford, UK
When:	May 5, 1957
Culprit:	Kenneth Barlow
Victim:	Elizabeth Barlow
Cause of death:	insulin overdose
Forensic technique:	toxicology

The Crime

The murderer's ideal poison would be broken down by the body so fast that by the time a post-mortem was carried out, there would be no remaining traces. Kenneth Barlow, a 38-year-old nurse working in a Bradford hospital, joked that insulin was the perfect murder weapon as it could not be traced afterward. When his second wife Elizabeth became pregnant, neither wanted a baby, so he injected her with ergometrine to cause a miscarriage, but repeated doses failed to work. Then, on the night of May 5, 1957, he found her dead in the bath. He told police that she had been unwell and had retired to bed after their evening meal. At 9:20 PM he found she had been sick, so he changed the bedding while she ran a bath. He then fell asleep, waking two hours later to find her lying in the water, and his vigorous efforts to apply artificial respiration were in vain.

The Case

The doctor called by Barlow had noticed that Elizabeth's pupils were dilated, and so had called the police. When the police inspected the scene, they noticed a small quantity of bath water trapped in the crooks of Elizabeth's arms, but none on the floor or on Barlow's pajamas. The signs suggested she had fallen deeply asleep and simply drifted off to her death in a semi-conscious state. Barlow himself described her symptoms as vomiting, weakness, sweating, and dilated pupils, all of which suggested extremely low, potentially fatal, blood sugar levels. This could have been caused by a massive injection of insulin, except that her blood sugar level was extremely high.

The Evidence

Barlow probably never knew of the recent research which showed that potentially fatal drops in blood sugar level could trigger an automatic response, causing the liver to release huge quantities of sugar into the blood. He was also unaware that lactic acid in the victim's body could greatly slow down insulin breakdown, which had been the case with Elizabeth. There was clearly still insulin in her body, though the level would have dropped since her death. Examiners from the Home Office Forensic Science Laboratory checked the body very carefully for the puncture marks of recent injections. They found two in each buttock, but Barlow insisted these were the sites of the ergometrine injections.

How could the investigators prove an insulin overdose had killed her? First they injected laboratory rats, mice, and guinea pigs with insulin. All showed similar symptoms and died quickly. Then they cut tissue samples from the sites of the injections on her body, and other groups of animals were injected with extracts from these tissues. They too died, showing the same symptoms of distress. In all, it took an astounding total of 150 rats, 24 guinea pigs, and 1,220 mice to provide sufficiently strong data of the dose administered to Elizabeth Barlow, who presumably thought the injections were to bring on the intended miscarriage. The evidence showed she had 84 units of insulin in her system when she died, suggesting a huge initial overdose of 240 units.

The Outcome

Barlow was tried at the end of July 1957, found guilty of his wife's murder, and given a life sentence. At the trial it emerged his first wife had died mysteriously just a year before, leaving him free to marry Elizabeth soon afterward. Had the new insulin data been available then, an earlier "perfect murder" might have been exposed in time.

Deadly Umbrella Attack

Where:	London, UK
When:	September 7, 1978
Culprits:	Bulgarian assassins
Victim:	Georgi Markov
Cause of death:	ricin poisoning
Forensic technique:	toxicology

The Crime

During the Cold War years, many dissidents from the Soviet Eastern European satellites found an apparently safe refuge in London. Some lived a quiet life in the West, but there were others who took a much more active role against their former masters. One of these was Georgi Markov, a Bulgarian who worked for the BBC World Service, broadcasting to his former homeland.

On the afternoon of Thursday September 7, 1978, Markov was waiting at a bus stop on Waterloo Bridge on the first stage of the routine journey back to his flat. He felt a sudden stabbing pain in his right leg, and turned round to see that he had been jabbed by the end of a furled umbrella carried by a passer-by. The man mumbled an apology, and rushed on to wave down a taxi.

When Markov reached his flat, he took a closer look at the site of the pain and found a small red puncture mark in the skin of his leg. Thinking it would soon disappear, he went to bed unconcerned by the mark. But by the following day, he was violently sick and his temperature had risen sharply. He was taken to hospital, where his now inflamed wound was X-rayed, and he was kept under observation.

The X-ray plates showed no signs of anything to account for his illness, but his condition rapidly deteriorated. His pulse was racing as his blood pressure plummeted. His temperature fell, but his white blood-cell count rose far above normal levels, and the doctors concluded he might be suffering from blood poisoning. He was given antibiotics, but before they could have any effect, he suffered severe convulsions. He sank into delirium and within three days he was dead.

The Case

Markov's body was given a detailed post-mortem examination, which revealed a tiny spherical pellet, only a millimeter or so across, buried beneath the skin. It had two very small holes drilled in it, but no sign remained of what it might have contained. The pellet was then sent to the Metropolitan Police forensic laboratory where it was analyzed and found to consist of an extremely tough alloy of platinum and iridium which would not show up under X-rays. It was probable that the holes in the pellet had held a very small amount of poison, but no trace remained. On the other hand, to produce such a violent and lethal reaction suggested this must have been something like a nerve agent, and that the pellet itself had been fired into the victim's leg by a gas gun hidden within the furled umbrella.

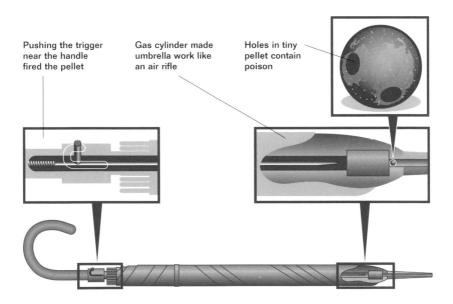

Pushing the trigger near the handle fired the pellet

Gas cylinder made umbrella work like an air rifle

Holes in tiny pellet contain poison

Above Possible mechanisms of the umbrella gun that is suspected to have shot the pellet containing deadly ricin into Markov's leg.

The Evidence

The sophistication of the method and the poison used suggested it was intelligence agents who were responsible, rather than criminal or terrorist groups. The most likely poison was thought to be ricin, developed from the seeds of the castor oil plant. On entering the bloodstream it causes the red corpuscles to mass together and then attacks the other body cells, producing vomiting and high temperature followed by falling blood pressure and eventually death from heart failure.

But could the microscopic dose of ricin contained in the pellet cause death so quickly? In the absence of any other proof, forensic experts carried out a comparison test. They injected a pig of similar size and weight to a mature human being, with the amount of ricin which could have been contained within the holes in the pellet. Not only did the pig die within 24 hours, but the symptoms and organ damage that it suffered were similar to those experienced by Markov.

The Outcome

Suspicion pointed directly at the Bulgarian regime, which issued firm official denials. However, another Bulgarian dissident, Vladimir Kostov, had suffered a similar attack in Paris the year before. In his case, an identical pellet had been fired into his back where it lodged in the muscle tissues, but failed to penetrate any of the main blood vessels, so he survived the attack. But the final outcome of the story had to wait for the fall of the Communist regime in Bulgaria in 1991, and admissions by the new rulers that their predecessors had commissioned and carried out assassination attempts against dissidents living in the West, including both Kostov and Markov.

Natural Causes or Murder?

Where:	New Jersey and Florida, USA
When:	1963–65
Culprit:	Carl Coppolino
Victims:	William Farber and Carmela Coppolino
Cause of death:	strangled and poisoned with succinylcholine chloride
Forensic technique:	toxicology

The Crime

Carl Coppolino and his wife Carmela were both doctors, originally practicing in New Jersey, where in 1962 they had struck up a close friendship with a neighboring couple, William and Marjorie Farber. In 1963, Carl took early retirement from his job as an anesthetist on the grounds of suffering heart problems, and he and Carmela decided to produce a book on alcoholism. That summer Farber died, and his death certificate was signed by Carmela, who ascribed the cause of death to coronary thrombosis. For the time being, Carmela continued with her medical practice, which left her husband free to spend more and more time with the recently widowed Marge.

The three continued as close friends, and in the spring of 1965 they moved to adjacent houses in Longboat Key, off the Florida resort of Sarasota. Then, on August 28, just four months after the move, Carmela also died. Carl explained she had suffered chest pains the day before, and her death was put down to heart failure. Within six weeks, Carl had married again, and moved to live with his new bride, a wealthy divorcee, while his own funds were augmented by a $65,000 insurance settlement he had made on Carmela shortly before she died. Finally, his old friend Marge Farber reported to police that there was something strange about Carmela's demise.

The Case

If Carmela had not died from heart failure, what could have caused her death? As an anesthetist, Carl Coppolino would be familiar with substances that could cause convincing symptoms of natural death and then disappear from the body before a post-mortem could be carried out. In particular, he could have used a powerful muscle relaxant called succinylcholine chloride, an overdose of which could kill within minutes, but would break down very quickly afterward. Could this have been administered to Carmela to cause her apparent and fatal heart attack?

The Evidence

Once again the proof depended on testing the compound on animals. The Chief Medical Examiner for Monmouth County in New Jersey, the area where the Coppolinos had practiced medicine, injected six rabbits with succinylcholine chloride and after they died buried them, having treated one with embalming fluid. A month later they were dug up and the bodies tested for the muscle relaxant. In all cases tests revealed succinic acid, a component of the drug, even though the drug itself had broken down long before. This enabled the investigators to have Carmela's body exhumed and also that of William Farber. Carmela's brain showed traces of succinic acid, which proved she had indeed been poisoned by succinylcholine chloride. Farber's body showed something even more surprising: his cricoid cartilage around the larynx was found to have been cracked in two places, a sure sign of death by strangulation. This was confirmed by his widow, who claimed that Carl Coppolino had strangled him when he and Marjorie were having an affair, prior to their move to Florida.

The Outcome

Carl Coppolino was tried separately for both murders. The defense was able to convince the jury there was no sign of bruising on Farber's throat and that the fractures of the cartilage could have been caused by clumsiness during the exhumation, while his heart was in poor enough condition to have been the cause of his death after all, and he was acquitted of that killing. But in the case of his wife's death, the detailed evidence produced a conviction of murder, though he was released on parole in 1979 after serving 12 years of his sentence.

The Fugitive Poisoner

Where:	London, UK
When:	January 31, 1910
Culprit:	Dr. Hawley Crippen
Victim:	Belle Elmore
Cause of death:	hyoscine poisoning
Forensic technique:	toxicology

The Crime

Dr. Hawley Harvey Crippen was born in Coldwater, Michigan in the USA in 1862. He qualified as a doctor and ophthalmologist before moving with his second wife, a music-hall singer with the stage name Belle Elmore, to London in 1900 to manage the UK office for an American patent medicine company. Unfortunately his qualifications were not recognized in England, but while business was poor, their expenses were high. He tried to augment their income by working as a dentist, but they depended heavily on Belle's money. Infatuated by the glamor of the theater, she had a series of open and flamboyant affairs, while keeping her husband under the tightest control. They rented a large Victorian house at 39 Hilldrop Crescent in Holloway, North London, and took in students, but Crippen returned home one day to find Belle in bed with one of the lodgers. The marriage finally fell apart, and Belle announced she was going to leave her husband, taking with her their joint savings. Soon after she disappeared from the London scene.

The Case

The day after Belle had given a dinner party at their house on January 31, 1910, Crippen announced to her music-hall friends that she had left him and returned to America with one of her lovers. In the meantime, he moved his secretary and mistress Ethel Le Neve into the house. But several of Belle's friends became suspicious when she was seen wearing items of Belle's jewelry. As the whispers became louder, the couple left London for Brussels and then Antwerp in Belgium, before taking a ship to North America. Crippen had told the police he had heard that Belle had died soon after arriving in

America, and had already been cremated, which aroused their suspicions even further. They had already searched the Hilldrop Crescent house once, and found nothing, but with the couple away, they returned and searched it three more times.

The Evidence

Only on the fourth search did they find the partial remains of a human body buried beneath the cellar floor, but it was impossible to establish the identity immediately as the head, limbs, and most of the skeleton were missing. Finally the Home Office pathologist Sir Bernard Spilsbury was able to establish that the remains were those of Belle from a patch of abdominal skin bearing a healed scar from an operation. He also found traces of hyoscine, a poison which produced symptoms resembling those of heart failure, but which was used by doctors in small doses to relieve anxiety and travel sickness. All this evidence pointed directly at Crippen, and police began to hunt for the fugitive couple.

The Outcome

They were already crossing the Atlantic on the steamship *Montrose*, posing as father and son. The captain became suspicious by their unduly affectionate behavior and went so far as to radio a message to the police back in England. There was just time for Chief Inspector Dew of Scotland Yard, who had originally questioned Crippen after Belle's disappearance, to catch a faster ship, which brought him to Canada before the *Montrose* docked. Posing as a Canadian pilot, he boarded the ship off the Canadian coast, and arrested the couple. Both were put on trial for Belle's murder—Ethel Le Neve was acquitted, but Crippen was found guilty and hanged. Had they decided to sail on an American ship direct to the USA rather than via Canada, Dew would have been powerless to arrest them and only long and elaborate extradition procedures could have brought Crippen, still an American citizen, back to his adopted country to stand trial.

Accidental Poisoning?

Where:	Gosport, Hampshire, UK
When:	July 22, 1955
Culprits:	John and Janet Armstrong
Victim:	Terence Armstrong
Cause of death:	overdose of Seconal tablets
Forensic technique:	toxicology

The Crime

John and Janet Armstrong's infant son, Terence, was only five months old
when he died on July 22, 1955 in Gosport, Hampshire, near the naval
hospital where his father served as a sick berth attendant. It seemed that he
had eaten the bright red berries of a laurel tree in the family's garden, under
which his pram had been left on the afternoon of his death. The post-
mortem showed his stomach contained red skins similar to the berries, and
the cause of this tragic and premature death appeared to be accidental—
except that his young parents had apparently been dogged by such
misfortune. Their other son, three-month-old Stephen, had died in the spring
of 1954, while their three-year-old daughter Pamela had been rushed to
hospital just two months before Terence's death with an unexplained but
serious illness that she only narrowly survived.

The Case

The parents seemed strangely indifferent to their loss. The pathologist who
had carried out the post-mortem, Dr. Harold Miller, had admittedly found
what at first appeared to be shells of laurel berries in the baby's throat and
stomach. He had placed one of these skins in a container of formaldehyde
and the rest of the baby's stomach contents in another bottle and left both in
the pathology laboratory refrigerator. When he examined them again later, he
found the skins had dissolved, which suggested they were not natural berries
at all.

The Evidence

Dr. Miller wasted no time in sending the samples, together with the baby's pillow and feeding bottle, to a specialist toxicology laboratory. They found that what had appeared to be berry skins were in reality traces of corn starch and a red dye called eosin. There was no trace of any berries, though there was no evidence of any identifiable poison either. On the other hand, the combination suggested to the doctor the red gelatin-covered tablets of a powerful barbiturate called Seconal, so as a check, he dissolved some tablets of the drug in gastric juices. They broke down to produce the same residue as his samples.

This in itself was not proof that little Terence had been fed Seconal, though even a small dose of the drug would have been enough to kill him, as well as explaining the symptoms leading up to his death: listlessness, difficulty in breathing, and a blue color to the face. Dr. Miller sent the samples to Scotland Yard's Forensic Laboratory where a long series of painstaking tests found minute samples of Seconal in the stomach contents and on the baby's pillow where he had vomited in his distress. Aware that the other two children had suffered similar symptoms in their illnesses, police exhumed the body of Stephen Armstrong, but found this was too decayed to reveal any specific poison in the remains. They also established that 50 Seconal tablets were missing from the hospital ward where John Armstrong worked, but there was still no proof Seconal tablets had been brought to the house and given to the baby.

The Outcome

The truth was finally revealed a year later, when Janet Armstrong gained a legal separation owing to her husband's cruelty. She then told police her husband had brought Seconal tablets home, and that after the baby's death, he had forced her to dispose of the rest of the tablets. Both were put on trial in November 1956 and each ended up blaming the other. Finally John Armstrong was sentenced to death for the murder of his son, and his wife was acquitted. A month later she admitted she had given Terence the fatal tablet, as the couple had decided they could not afford to have any more children, but her husband's sentence had by then been changed to life imprisonment.

Polonium Trail

Where: London, UK
When: November 2006
Culprit: as yet unsolved
Victim: Alexander Litvinenko
Cause of death: polonium poisoning
Forensic technique: toxicology

The Crime

Alexander Litvinenko was a prominent Russian defector living in London with his wife and teenage son. He had formerly worked for the KGB before the break-up of the Soviet Union, but had come under fierce criticism for failing to purge the intelligence service of corruption and links to organized crime. Since moving to the West, he had become an increasingly vocal critic of the leadership of Russian President Vladimir Putin, over what he saw as

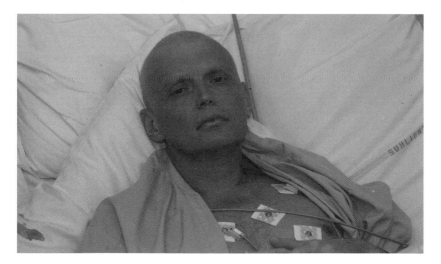

Above Alexander Litvinenko at the Intensive Care Unit of University College Hospital in London, England, on November 20, 2006.

the erosion of freedom in his homeland. His outspoken claims of the Russian government's complicity in the deaths of other dissidents brought him an increasingly high-profile role in the London expatriate community, and he was known to have concerns about the possibility of action against him by the FSB, the KGB's successor as the Russian intelligence service.

The Case

On November 11, 2006, he was due to meet an Italian academic named Mario Scaramella at a Japanese sushi bar called Itsu. He planned to hand Scaramella information on the shooting of investigative journalist Anna Politovskaya in Moscow, and also to discuss rumors that both Litvinenko and Scaramella had appeared on a current FSB hit list. Later that day, he was due to meet three Russian contacts in the Pine Bar of the Millennium Hotel: Vyacheslav Sokolenko, Dmitri Kowtun, and Andrei Lugovoi, a former KGB colleague. Both meetings appeared to run according

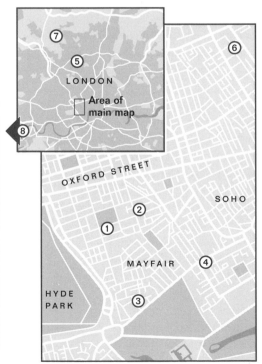

Trail of polonium traces

1. Millenium Hotel
2. 25 Grosvenor Street
3. 7 Down Street
4. Itsu Sushi Bar
5. Osier Crescent, Muswell Hill
6. University College Hospital
7. Barnet Hospital
8. Heathrow Airport

to plan, but that evening at his home in Muswell Hill, Litvinenko felt increasingly ill and was repeatedly sick. He was taken to hospital after three days of increasing stomach pains, where his condition continued to deteriorate. Three weeks after the onset of his mysterious symptoms, he was dead.

The Evidence

Tests on Litvinenko's body showed the presence of a highly toxic and unusual substance in his urine: polonium-210, a strong emitter of lethal alpha radiation if absorbed into a victim's body through the contamination of food or drink. Police found traces of the material at his home, and at the sites of both meetings. The net was spread more widely as traces showed up at both hospitals where Litvinenko had been treated, at the London office of exiled Russian business tycoon Boris Berezovsky, and on two airliners which had carried out flights between Moscow and London. The use of polonium-210 carried several implications—it is quick and effective, but very easy to smuggle as its radiation is easily contained except when taken into the body. And it is almost impossible to procure, except for someone with the official power to obtain supplies from a nuclear power station or another working reactor.

The Outcome

At first, because of the contamination at the sushi bar, Scaramella came under suspicion until it emerged that Litvinenko had had a meeting with his Russian contacts there two weeks earlier. All the other signs therefore pointed to the Russian government, or at least the FSB, as they had the classic trilogy of motive (silencing an outspoken critic), the means (access to nuclear reactors), and the opportunity (spiking Litvinenko's food or drink with the poison at one of several meetings). Furthermore, the Russian intelligence services have a long track record in assassinating those seen as enemies of the state, in a range of overseas countries. Meanwhile, applications have been made to extradite Andrei Lugovoi, but the Russians have refused, on the grounds that their constitution expressly forbids the extradition of Russian citizens. Lugovoi and his colleagues insist they are innocent of any involvement in the death of Litvinenko, and the affair promises to cause a deeper than usual chill in Anglo-Russian relations.

Fallen Tycoon

Where:	at sea, south-west of Spain
When:	November 5, 1991
Culprit:	accidental death
Victim:	Robert Maxwell
Cause of death:	accidental drowning
Forensic technique:	forensic biology

The Crime

The flamboyant Robert Maxwell had come to dominate the British and US media industries, having built up huge and lucrative holdings in newspapers and publishing which funded the most lavish of lifestyles. Born Jan Ludvik Hoch in Czechoslovakia in 1923, his shadowy past ensured he was followed by every kind of rumor, from a heroic wartime career to involvement in the murky world of espionage through links with the Israeli intelligence service Mossad, and he had made a host of enemies during the course of his life. He had served in the British Army and later become a Labour MP for six years, though his publishing empire appeared to stand on ever shakier foundations.

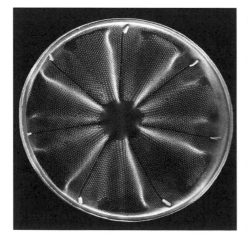

The Case

In November 1991, he was cruising south-west of Spain aboard his huge motor-yacht the *Lady Ghislaine*. He was last seen on deck before retiring at the end of the evening of the 5th. The next morning, the crew of the vessel could find no sign of him, and a widespread search was begun. His body was finally found

Left A diatom viewed under a microscope.

12 hours later, floating in the sea off the Canary Islands, and immediately the speculation began: had he fallen, or was he pushed?

The Evidence

Maxwell had vanished overboard while the vessel was in Spanish territorial waters, so the investigation fell to the Spanish authorities. The distinction should have been relatively simple: if he had been assassinated, it seemed highly likely he would have been dead on entering the water. If he had fallen into the sea, he would have been alive on hitting the water, and there should have been clear evidence of drowning. In fact, the distinction was blurred, entirely in accord with Maxwell's often mysterious life and history.

There is a simple test: when a person drowns, microscopic organisms called diatoms, which exist in both salt and fresh water, are absorbed into the body tissues along with the water. When tissue samples are dissolved in acid, the silica skeletons of diatoms can clearly be seen under a microscope. Maxwell's blood and body tissues showed the presence of diatoms, and this at least was evidence he had been alive when he hit the water, and had drowned soon afterward. Moreover, the post-mortem showed no other signs of injuries to suggest he had been attacked and pushed over the rail while still alive. However, his lungs were not full of sea water, as they normally would be in a drowning victim. Instead, the investigators concluded he had been a victim of a condition called "dry drowning"—a spasm of the larynx caused by the shock of hitting the water, bringing about a huge increase in blood pressure and causing the heart to stop.

The Outcome

The balance of probabilities seemed to show Maxwell had not been the victim of a murder attempt. What was impossible to prove was whether he lost his balance, and accidentally fell across the rail and into the water, or whether his growing business problems prompted him to end his life. Certainly his death caused the collapse of his business empire, and the emergence of certain details, like the looting of company pension funds, effectively destroyed what was left of his reputation and ended in his sons standing trial for fraud over decisions taken in running Maxwell's companies.

Body in a Trunk

Where:	Paris, France
When:	July 27, 1889
Culprits:	Michel Eyraud and Gabrielle Bompard
Victim:	Toussaint-Augsent Gouffé
Cause of death:	strangled
Forensic technique:	pathology

The Crime

On July 27, 1889, a Parisian bailiff named Toussaint-Augsent Gouffé was reported missing. On August 15 a roadmender passing through the hamlet of Millery, ten miles south of Lyon, noticed a terrible smell rising from the bushes along the riverbank. There he found a badly decomposed body, tied up in a cloth. The corpse was taken to the morgue in Lyon, but there was nothing to reveal its identity. When the find was reported to the head detective of the Paris police, M. Goron, he thought this might be Gouffé, and the missing man's brother-in-law went to identify the remains. He did not recognize the corpse but as its hair and beard was black, it could not be Gouffé, who had bright chestnut-colored hair. Two days later the remains of a cabin trunk were found nearby, also smelling of decomposition, with a label showing it had been sent by train from Paris to Lyon on the day Gouffé had been reported missing, and a key found near the body fitted the lock.

The Case

The corpse was already buried when Goron visited Lyon, but the pathologist had kept some of the victim's black hair; when this was rinsed in distilled water, the black dissolved, revealing a natural chestnut color. Goron was then able to have the body exhumed and re-examined. A defect of the right knee, together with a missing tooth and an old ankle injury, proved it was Gouffé. It also showed he had been strangled.

But who had killed him? A colleague revealed that another person with links to the bankruptcy world, one Michel Eyraud, had disappeared from

Paris at the same time with his mistress, Gabrielle Bompard. The police reassembled the trunk and put it on show in the city morgue. At the end of the year a letter arrived from a boarding-house keeper in London's Gower Street, who said that Eyraud and Bompard had stayed there in July. In addition, it was revealed that two people matching their descriptions had bought a trunk in a shop in Euston Road before returning to France.

The Evidence

In January 1890 Goron had a letter from Eyraud in New York, protesting his innocence and blaming his former mistress. The very next day, Bompard reported to the Paris police, but merely put the blame on Eyraud. She was arrested and agents were sent to track down the missing Eyraud, who was eventually discovered in Havana and brought back to Paris to appear before the examining magistrate on July 1, 1890, almost a year after the murder.

The couple admitted they were destitute, and had planned for Bompard to lure a victim to a secluded apartment where they would kill and rob him. They found a ground-floor flat in the Rue Tronson-Ducoudray and, on their London visit, bought the trunk, a pulley, a length of rope, and some canvas, which Bompard sewed into a bag to contain the corpse. The pulley was fixed to a cross beam above the bed, and they chose their victim with care. Eyraud and Gouffé had a friend in common who revealed that on Friday nights Gouffé would try to pick up a woman to spend the night with. This would make it fairly easy for Bompard to lure him to the flat. There Eyraud would hide behind a curtain, and when Gouffé was distracted he would slip the rope around his neck, and haul him up over the pulley until he was throttled.

The Outcome

The murder went according to plan, but they found little of value on the corpse. Eyraud went to Gouffé's office but missed 14,000 francs hidden under papers. All they could do was strip the body, place it into the bag, and lock it in the trunk. It was then sent to Lyon where they collected it, dumped the body and the trunk, and fled to America before it was discovered. Each blamed the other for the decisive role in murdering Gouffé. Bompard was finally sentenced to 20 years in prison, and Eyraud was executed.

Part Two:
Fire and
Explosions

Time-delayed Blaze

Where:	New Hampshire, USA
When:	September 28, 1916
Culprit:	Frank Small
Victim:	Florence Small
Cause of death:	shot, strangled, beaten
Forensic technique:	pathology

The Crime

Murderers often try to provide an alibi to cover up their crimes. One of the most elaborate attempts to do this was developed by an unsuccessful businessman, Frederick Small, who had retired to a cottage in Mountainview, on the shore of Lake Ossipee in New Hampshire, with his wife Florence.

Small made regular business trips to Boston to oversee what was left of their savings. His final trip was on September 28, 1916. A local carrier named George Kennett came to the house to run Small to the station to catch the 4 PM train to Boston. Normally Kennett would have a drink when he came by, but this time Small called goodbye to his wife as he closed the house door, and they left immediately. At the station he met an acquaintance, Edwin Conner, who was traveling to the city with him. When they arrived, Small checked into a hotel, sent a postcard to his wife, and then both men went to a cinema. When they returned to the hotel, Small was told that there had been a fire at his cottage, and it had been impossible to rescue his wife. The two men hired a car and drove through the night to reach the scene.

The Case

The blaze had been extremely intense, but when investigators were finally able to enter the ruins, they found that Florence's corpse had fallen through into the cellar as the floor planks had collapsed. Because conditions there were cooler and damper than in the rest of the cottage, her body had not been entirely consumed by the flames. Her face and trunk had remained relatively intact, and they showed she had been shot, strangled, and severely beaten. Neighbors testified that Small had a history of violence towards his wife, while police found he had taken out a $20,000 insurance policy on his wife and another $3,000 on the cottage. However, the fact he was more than a hundred miles away when the fire began seemed enough to absolve him.

The Evidence

Only when the investigators searched the ashes of the cottage did Small's alibi begin to collapse. They found a .32 piston, which belonged to Small, and the remains of a small alarm clock with wires and a spark device attached. Local traders' records showed five gallons of kerosene had been delivered to the cottage earlier on the day of the fire, and the medical examiner noticed a strange coating on Florence's body made up of the residue of a welding material called thermite, containing highly inflammable substances like aluminium and magnesium which would burn at a very high temperature if set alight. Finally, at Florence's post-mortem, analysis of the contents of her stomach showed the meal she was known to have eaten at midday was still undigested. In other words, she had been killed long before 10 PM that evening, when the fire had started.

The Outcome

Small was put on trial for the murder of his wife. He claimed she had been the victim of a passing attacker, but the remains of his apparently ingenious alibi finally crumbled away when a local mechanic was commissioned to use items identical to those found in the ashes to set up a timed fire-raising device. It was shown to the court to work perfectly in setting off an intense blaze after a preset delay. Small was found guilty, sentenced to death, and hanged in early 1918.

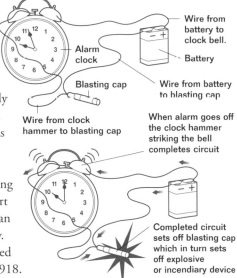

Wire from battery to clock bell.

Alarm clock

Battery

Blasting cap

Wire from battery to blasting cap

Wire from clock hammer to blasting cap

When alarm goes off the clock hammer striking the bell completes circuit

Completed circuit sets off blasting cap which in turn sets off explosive or incendiary device

A Matter of Inheritance

Where:	Naples, Florida, USA
When:	July 9, 1985
Culprit:	Steven Benson
Victims:	Margaret and Scott Benson
Cause of death:	car bomb
Forensic technique:	fingerprinting

The Crime

The Benson family lived in Naples, in the southern part of Florida, enjoying an enviable lifestyle based on the profits made from Lancaster Leaf, a tobacco company founded by the father of widowed Margaret Benson. But all was not well with the Benson family, and Margaret had become increasingly worried about the behavior of her 35-year-old son Steven, who had a string of failed and expensive business ventures behind him. She was already convinced he had started to steal money from her, and she feared his desperate need for funds might lead to more violent action. In the summer of 1985, she asked the family lawyer to investigate Steven's affairs. Within days, she and her younger adopted son Scott had been blown to pieces while sitting in the family station wagon outside their house.

The Case

The facts seemed straightforward enough. Steven Benson was marking out a site for a new home, and had driven the 1978 Chevrolet Suburban to his grandmother's house to pick up the materials he needed. He called at a local store for coffee and rolls, which he took back to the family house for breakfast. At 9 PM his mother, brother, and his sister Carol Lynn were in the car ready to travel out to the site with him. Steven said he had left his tape measure in the house, and went to fetch it. He threw the ignition keys to Scott and told him he could start up the car, ready for the drive. As Steven walked into the house, Scott turned the ignition key and the car exploded with enormous force. Margaret and Scott were killed instantly, and only Carol Lynn survived, though she was severely injured.

The Evidence

Steven's apparent lack of concern at the violent deaths of his mother and adopted brother, not to mention the serious injuries to his sister, triggered deep suspicion on the part of the investigators. Could he have devised some kind of explosive device to wreck the car, kill his family, and leave him as the sole inheritor of a multi-million dollar fortune? After a painstaking search of the wreckage of the vehicle, they found fragments of galvanized metal pipe that had been used as the bomb casing. The ends of the pipe had been sealed by a pair of threaded end caps, both of which were intact, and their markings showed that one had been made by a company called Grinnell, the other by Union Brand. Also found in the wreckage were four small 1.5 volt batteries, a switch, and a fragment of circuit board which definitely did not belong in the car's electrical system.

Teams of detectives toured local hardware stores, scrap yards, and building sites to check where the pipe and end caps had come from. Finally, they found a store where records showed a pair of threaded end caps had been bought just four days before the killings, and the assistant who dealt with the sale thought he remembered a man matching Steven Benson's description. The sales documentation was treated for fingerprints, and one of them showed a clear palm print which proved to be that of Steven Benson.

The Outcome

On August 21, 1985, Steven Benson was arrested for the murder of his mother and brother. Financial checks showed he had indeed been stealing from his mother, and was worried she would discover what was going on, and disinherit him from his share of the family wealth as a result. He was finally tried the following year. The defense tried to pin responsibility on Scott, who it emerged was really the illegitimate son of Carol Lynn but adopted by her mother. Scott had been involved with drugs, but the jury still found Steven guilty of both killings.

Sabotage or Suicide

Where:	Caribbean Sea
When:	April 19, 1989
Culprit:	accident
Victims:	47 sailors
Cause of death:	explosion
Forensic technique:	ballistics

The Crime

Each of the four huge battleships of the *Missouri* class of the US Navy carried nine 16-inch guns in three triple turrets, which could fire a high explosive projectile weighing a ton and a quarter up to 24 miles (38 km). To propel the huge shells, the turret crews had to load different combinations of bagged nitro-cellulose explosive charges into the breech of the gun behind the shell.

USS Iowa was carrying out a practice firing on April 19, 1989 when explosive charges being loaded into the breech of the center gun of number two turret suddenly detonated. The explosion sent a blast back through the turret, killing 47 sailors, including the entire turret crew. Navy investigators had to determine whether the disaster was accidental or sabotage.

The Case

The gun had not been fired earlier, so there was no heat build-up, and the first enquiry established that a spontaneous explosion in a cold barrel had never occurred in the history of the Navy. Investigators found traces of steel wool, calcium hypochlorite, and brake fluid inside the barrel. Could they be remains of a device placed there to set off the charges? The captain of the center gun, Clayton Hartwig, was rumored to have had a relationship with a sailor in the turret crew, and had been in control of the loading operation. Both men died in the tragedy; could it have beeen a bizarre act of suicide or revenge?

The Evidence

A second technical enquiry was carried out by explosives experts. First, they checked the gun-turrets of the *Iowa*'s sister ships, where they found similar traces of steel fibers, calcium, and chlorine in barrels that had been fired with no trouble. Tests showed they are found in cleaning fluids and lubricants used in turret maintenance, or in sea water, and were not evidence of sabotage.

One factor separated the loading of the center gun from those on either side, which functioned normally. The power-driven rammer which forced the bagged charges into the breech pushed them two feet (0.6 m) further than it should have done, and with greater force. But explosive charges remain stable under heavy provocation. Setting light to the explosive with a cigarette lighter took nine minutes, and dropping the charges from heights of up to 100 feet (30 m) caused no problem.

Then the experts examined the "trim bags"—additional bags of explosive inserted into the main charges to correct weight variations. Unlike the main charges, the explosives in the smaller bags were not tightly packed, making them potentially more susceptible to the shock of over-ramming when the gun was loaded. They set up a test rig and dropped a series of charges to replicate these effects. Nothing happened on 17 successive tests, but when it was dropped for the 18th time, the charge was loaded with fewer trim-charge pellets with wider gaps between them and this time the charge finally detonated and blew the test rig apart.

The Outcome

Supplied with an explanation of a technical fault for the explosion, the Navy was able to take positive action in changing the loading procedures for its biggest guns, and no more firing mishaps were ever identified.

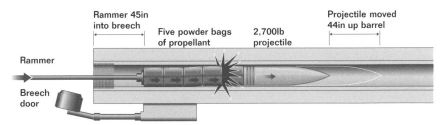

Above The explosion is thought to have been accidental, caused by the charges being pushed too far into the breech and then being over-rammed.

Tragedy of Flight 103

Where:	Lockerbie, Scotland
When:	December 21, 1988
Culprit:	Abdelbaset Ali Mohmed Al Megrahi
Victims:	270 victims
Cause of death:	bomb on an aeroplane
Forensic technique:	ballistics

The Crime

At just after 7 PM on the evening of December 21, 1988, a Pan American Boeing 747 was flying at 31,000 feet (9 km) over Western Scotland en route from London to New York when its echo disappeared from ground control radar screens. The huge aircraft broke up in mid-air and the largest pieces fell on the small town of Lockerbie below, where they hit the ground with the force of a minor earthquake. In all, 259 people aboard the aircraft and 11 people on the ground died in the tragedy.

The Case

Because the aircraft had been traveling at speed when it broke up, fragments of wreckage were spread out across a huge area of the Scottish countryside, in two distinct trails. The first step in determining the cause of the aircraft breaking up was to collect as many pieces as possible, to isolate the evidence of how this terrible disaster had occurred. It was an enormous task, tracing more than four million fragments of wreckage spread over approximately a thousand square miles (2590 km^2). All were brought to a reassembly hangar in a military depot near Carlisle, for a two-dimensional reconstruction, fitting each part of the aircraft into the right relationship with its neighbors in the 747's structure.

From the beginning, investigators found worrying anomalies. The pieces of the after baggage hold had fallen in a fairly restricted area, whereas those of the forward hold were far more scattered, suggesting this had been one of the first parts of the aircraft to break up. This implied a bomb may have been

Above The full reconstruction of 1988 terrorist bomb-blasted Pan Am flight 103 plane, which exploded over Lockerbie, Scotland.

placed in the hold, and when closer examination revealed two of the cargo containers placed in the forward hold showed clear signs of explosive damage, the suspicion was confirmed. Then the discovery of a tiny fragment of printed circuit board, forced into a crease of the container paneling by the blast of the explosion, was traced to a particular model of Toshiba radio/cassette player, which must have contained the explosive. Other fragments showed the device had been hidden in a brown suitcase which had been loaded into the container so that it was against the plane's outer skin.

The Evidence

The aircraft parts were then sent to the Royal Aircraft Establishment at Farnborough for a full three-dimensional reconstruction to determine the break-up sequence. For example, the noise of the bomb exploding was heard on the cockpit voice recorder moments before a complete power failure stopped the recording. And parts of the cables which held the curtains that screened the baggage container were found in one of the engine air intakes, showing that the forward fuselage had burst open while the engines were still running normally.

To determine the amount of explosive involved, armament experts placed different amounts of explosive in identical cassette radios and detonated them in identical luggage containers. Through comparing the damage with the explosive damage shown by the containers aboard the aircraft, they were able to deduce that just 2.2 pounds (1 kg) of explosive had been enough. In determining who was responsible for the disaster, the rest of the investigation was a triumph of forensic detection—the position of the cassette in the hold showed it had been transferred from a connecting flight from Frankfurt before the 747 had taken off from London. Clothing fibers also found in the luggage were traced to items bought in Malta and flown to Frankfurt the day before, and enquiries on the island later traced them to unnamed Libyans.

The Outcome

Finally, a case was brought against the Libyan intelligence services, and under pressure of economic sanctions, the Libyan government finally identified two of their agents, Al Amin Khalifa Fhimah and Abdelbaset Ali Mohmed Al Megrahi, as the men responsible. They were put on trial in Holland, at a special court held under Scottish laws, representing the country where the victims had died. On January 31, 2001, after a nine-month trial, Fhimah was acquitted but Megrahi was found guilty of the murders and he was sentenced to life imprisonment, to be served in Glasgow's Barlinnie prison.

Clues in the Ruins

Where: Oklahoma, USA
When: April 19, 1995
Culprit: Timothy McVeigh
Victims: 168 victims
Cause of death: bomb exploding
Forensic technique: explosions analysis

The Crime

Most people responsible for the death of a victim would try to disguise the result of their deliberate and violent actions. If the deaths of their victims can be made to appear as tragic accidents, so much the better. But the minds of terrorists march to an entirely different beat. They crave publicity for their acts, so it is essential they appear deliberate from the beginning, though if those responsible can disguise their identities, then they are free to plan more lethal acts of violence. On April 19, 1995, the large multi-story Alfred P. Murrah Federal Building in the center of Oklahoma City was blown apart by a massive bomb, killing a total of 168 people, many of them children in a day-care center within the building.

The Case

With such a huge explosion and death toll on their hands, investigators were set the challenge of having to search for the smallest pieces of evidence amid thousands of tons of rubble and wreckage. On this occasion, though, they had the extraordinary good fortune to find a vital clue early on in the process, with the discovery of a piece of twisted metal which was identified as part of the axle of a van, almost certainly the vehicle which had carried the bomb. Even more encouraging was the fact that the part carried a partial vehicle identification number, which enabled the van to be traced. When investigators checked in the vehicle database maintained by the National Crime Insurance Bureau, they found it was a 1993 Ford, operated by a hire company, Ryder Rentals of Miami, but that this particular vehicle had been hired from the company's Junction City, Kansas branch.

The Evidence

Finding the people who had hired the van required a step back to old-fashioned detective work. Ryder staff at Junction City helped police produce sketches of the two men who had hired the van and teams of investigators began interviewing staff at all the hotels, restaurants, diners, and fuel stops between Junction City and Oklahoma City to see if anyone remembered seeing either man. Lee MacGown, manager of the Dreamland Hotel in Junction City, recalled seeing one of the men depicted, who had used the alias "Kling" when hiring the van, but who signed the register as Timothy McVeigh. On the assumption that this was his real name, police started to track him down, only to find he was already under arrest. A highway patrol officer had flagged down McVeigh's battered yellow Mercury Marquis because of a missing license plate. McVeigh was found to be trying to conceal a semi-automatic pistol, and he was put under arrest and taken to Noble County Jail. The Michigan address shown on his driver's license was checked and found to be the home of Terry Nichols, who turned out to be the second suspect. Bomb experts estimated the damage done to the building would have taken some 4,000 pounds (1,800 kg) of a mixture of ammonium nitrate fertilizer and fuel oil, both of which are easily obtainable ingredients. Fragments of the barrels which had held the explosive, found at the site of the explosion, had markings similar to barrels found at Nichols' home, and traces of the explosives were found on the clothing of both suspects.

The Outcome

Timothy McVeigh and Terry Nichols were put on trial for the Oklahoma bombing. In June 1997, McVeigh was found guilty on all charges and sentenced to death by lethal injection. Nichols, who was seen as an accomplice rather than the prime agent for the killings, was given life imprisonment. McVeigh's lawyers mounted a succession of appeals, all the way to the US Supreme Court, but all proved unsuccessful and he was executed on June 11, 2001 in the Federal prison at Terre Haute, Indiana.

Right Rescue workers at the ruins of the Alfred P. Murrah Federal Building in Oklahoma City.

Part Three:

Fingerprints,
Blood, and
Ballistics

The Persistent Print

Where:	Chicago, USA
When:	December 8, 1951
Culprit:	George Ross
Victim:	Forney L. "Whitey" Haas
Cause of death:	gunshot wounds
Forensic technique:	fingerprinting

The Crime

On December 8, 1951 a police patrol car driver on the east side of Chicago, in the area near the Statler Hotel, spotted a Lincoln driving the wrong way down a one-way street. The car had out-of-state California plates and when he chased it and forced it to stop, the driver apologized and said he was not used to the area. But Patrolman Forney L. "Whitey" Haas had 17 years of experience behind him, and he asked to see his driver's license. The other man said it was back at his boarding house, and Haas thought it worth checking. They drove to the address, 8120 Euclid Avenue, and went up to the man's room. The landlady, Mrs. Lottie Cooper, heard the sounds of a loud argument at around 1:30 AM, followed by three gunshots. A man then pushed past her and out through the front door. Patrolman Haas was found on the stairs with wounds in his head, chest, and left arm and was taken to Mount Sinai Hospital, where he was pronounced dead on arrival.

The Case

The first step was to identify his killer. The Lincoln had been stolen in California, where it had been involved in a series of robberies. One of the suspects was a 27-year-old criminal named George Ross. Mrs. Cooper was shown a picture of Ross from police files, and confirmed it was the man who had rented a room from her under the name of Montgomery, and who had pushed past her carrying a revolver on the night of the shooting. Meanwhile, by this time, Ross himself had reached Cleveland, where he realized he had to get rid of the murder weapon. He went to the washroom in a roadside diner and flushed the pistol down the toilet. He then went on the run, only to be caught in Maryland nine days later after being recognized by a farmer who gave him a lift. On the way he had dropped another revolver which was shown not to be the murder weapon.

The Evidence

Ross was put on trial for the murder of Forney Haas on February 4, 1952. At the heart of the evidence against him was the murder weapon—Haas' own gun. A customer at the diner in Cleveland had complained that the toilet appeared to be blocked, and the obstruction was found to be a revolver, caught in a bend in the waste pipe. Police checked the serial number and found it was the missing gun. The next step was to check it for Ross' fingerprints, although normally all traces would have been washed away after being left in water for so long. But to their unbounded surprise, after the inevitable disappointment of finding no prints on either the butt or the trigger, they found a clear and identifiable print, belonging to Ross, clearly visible on the barrel.

The Outcome

This was the first time such a thing had happened. The print was so clear and durable it seemed almost to have been burned into the metal. Various theories were advanced to account for this: perhaps the print had reacted with copper in the water from the ball valve in the toilet tank, or with the heavy lime content of the local water, or maybe from the excessive salt content of Ross' own sweat when he had left the print. Whatever the explanation, something had caused proof of his identity to be etched into the murder weapon, and this was enough to convict him and send him to the electric chair on January 16, 1953.

A Mass Fingerprinting

Where:	Blackburn, Lancashire, UK
When:	September 15, 1948
Culprit:	Peter Griffiths
Victim:	Julie Anne Devaney
Cause of death:	blows to the head
Forensic technique:	fingerprinting

The Crime

In the Lancashire town of Blackburn at 1:20 AM on September 15, 1948, the night nurse in one of the children's wards at Queen's Park Hospital was making her rounds when she noticed that one of her six charges, three-year-old Julie Anne Devaney, was missing. Next to the empty cot was a large glass Winchester bottle containing sterile water, but nothing else out of the ordinary. The police were called, and the hospital grounds were searched, where they found the little girl's body just an hour and a half after the alarm was raised. She had been sexually assaulted and had suffered heavy blows to the head.

The Case

Finding the identity of the killer depended on the meager physical evidence left behind at the scene. As well as the Winchester bottle, which carried several sets of fingerprints, there were faint traces of footprints in the highly waxed surface of the ward floor, which showed the killer had taken off his shoes to avoid making too much noise. Although there was nothing about the prints to unmask the killer, they did show he had walked to three of the cots before reaching that of Julie, and had picked up the bottle on the way. He had then placed it on the floor before picking her up and making his escape, so one set of the fingerprints on the bottle was almost certainly his.

The Evidence

Police decided that only someone with local knowledge could have found a way into the ward, and pick out the hiding place for the girl's body in the grounds in complete darkness. So they began the first mass fingerprinting of

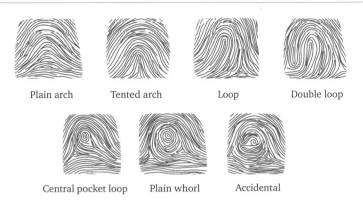

Plain arch   Tented arch   Loop   Double loop

Central pocket loop   Plain whorl   Accidental

Above The seven main classifications of fingerprint.

the population on a truly heroic scale. First they compared the prints on the bottle with everyone with a legitimate reason to be in the ward at any time. These alone amounted to 642, but finally they eliminated all but one set of prints on the bottle, which had to be those of the killer. Next, they fingerprinted every male over the age of 16 who had been in the town the night of the murder. After two months, more than 45,000 sets of prints had been taken and checked, but none were found to match those on the bottle.

The Outcome

Police had so far worked with identity cards, still in use after the war years, and the electoral register. Now they switched to another wartime measure still in operation—the ration books which gave every citizen access to essential foodstuffs. When police checked the records of the issue of ration books in Blackburn against their fingerprint records, they found as many as 200 people had not been checked. Among the missing suspects was a 22-year-old man named Peter Griffiths, an ex-soldier now working in a local flourmill. His prints were the 46,253rd set to be taken and they were a perfect match for those on the bottle. His stockinged feet were the right size to match casts taken of the tracks found in the ward, and fibers from the girl's nightgown were found on his clothes. He was tried and convicted of murder, and went to the gallows almost six months to the day after the death of his victim.

Poisoned Painkillers

Where:	Seattle, USA
When:	June 11, 1986
Culprit:	Stella Nickell
Victims:	Susan Snow and Bruce Nickell
Cause of death:	cyanide poisoning
Forensic technique:	chemical tracing

The Crime

On the morning of June 11, 1986 Seattle bank employee Susan Snow had a persistent headache. Before leaving for work, she took two Excedrin extra-strength painkiller tablets. Soon afterwards, she collapsed and paramedics took her to hospital, where she died later that morning. At her post-mortem, an assistant noticed a smell of bitter almonds, which raised suspicions of cyanide poisoning, and tests confirmed this. The logical explanation was that the painkillers had been contaminated with this deadliest of poisons, and when checked, cyanide traces were found in the remaining tablets.

This seemed like a case of product tampering. The US Food and Drug Administration (FDA) and manufacturers Bristol-Myers issued recall notices for that batch of tablets. In the meantime, Seattle police checked local stores in the immediate area, and two more contaminated packs were found—one in the suburb where Susan Snow had lived, and the other a few miles away. The very next day, they were contacted by Stella Nickell, a recently widowed 42-year-old, whose husband Bruce had taken the same tablets 12 days earlier, and collapsed and died soon afterward. Could there be any connection?

The Case

Checks showed two packs of Excedrin painkillers in Stella Nickell's home both contained cyanide traces. By then, searches over the north-western USA had turned up only five contaminated packages, yet she insisted the two packets had been bought on different days from different stores. The odds against this defied any rational explanation, and Stella Nickell moved from victim to potential suspect. Could she have contaminated the bottles to kill her husband? And were the pills that killed Susan Snow part of a plot to suggest a case of tampering, so she could sue the manufacturers in her role as victim? She and her husband had been considered a close and devoted couple and she had seemed grief-stricken by his death, but closer checks revealed worrying flaws.

The Evidence

The FBI forensic laboratory checked the contaminated capsules more closely. Every one contained microscopic traces of a specialized chemical used to kill algae in tropical fish tanks. They finally identified a particular product called Algae Destroyer, and concluded the only reason for its presence was cross contamination, caused by the perpetrator of the crime preparing the cyanide in a container previously used to crush Algae Destroyer capsules.

There was still no positive link with Stella Nickell, but on August 25, detectives checking local pet supply stores found an assistant who identified Stella Nickell as a customer who had bought Algae Destroyer some weeks earlier. Police already knew the Nickells kept tropical fish, but at this stage the evidence was not conclusive enough to bring a case. Even when they discovered that the couple had been deeply in debt, and that Bruce had been heavily insured (though most of the benefits would only have been paid if he had died as the result of an accident, or a deliberate crime, like the contamination of medicines), Stella maintained her angry denials of any responsibility for his death.

The Outcome

Finally, one of the couple's daughters revealed she had heard her mother talk of killing her husband, and saying that cyanide might do the job very well, even researching the poison in books from local libraries. Agents found she had failed to return a book on poisons from the Auburn library and had been sent an overdue notice for another book on poisonous plants. The book was traced and found to have been issued to her twice, shortly before her husband's death. Fingerprint checks revealed 84 of her prints, most on the pages dealing with cyanide. Stella Nickell was charged with murder and product tampering, and on May 9, 1988 was sentenced to a total of 90 years in prison.

Bloodstained Carpenter

Where:	Gohren, Rugen, Germany
When:	July 1, 1901
Culprit:	Ludwig Tessnow
Victims:	Hermann and Peter Stubbe
Cause of death:	blows to the head
Forensic technique:	serology

The Crime

Today's forensic scientists have a formidable battery of tests and techniques
for unraveling the secrets of a crime scene. Yet just over a century ago, it was
impossible to even determine whether apparent bloodstains really were
human blood. In the case of two young German brothers, eight-year-old
Hermann and six-year-old Peter Stubbe, catching their killer depended on the
first use of a reliable test. On the afternoon of July 1, 1901 the brothers had
failed to return to the family home in a village called Gohren on the island of
Rugen on the Baltic coast of northern Germany.

The next day, searchers found their dismembered bodies scattered in
nearby woods. The skulls were smashed, Hermann's heart was missing, and a
jagged and bloodstained stone found nearby was almost certainly the murder
weapon. There was even a potential suspect: a fruit seller had seen a local
carpenter talking to the boys on the afternoon they vanished. He was an
oddly behaved, reclusive man named Ludwig Tessnow, who lived in a nearby
village called Baabe. Police searched his home and workshop, and found
clothes and boots bearing dark stains, though the clothes had just been
thoroughly washed. Tessnow explained that the marks were simply wood dye
used in his work and the police, unable to prove otherwise, had no grounds
for charging him.

The Case

Under the German legal system, cases are first pursued by the local examining
magistrate, in this case a man named Johann Schmidt. He recalled a
strikingly similar case on September 8, 1898 in the village of Lechtingen,

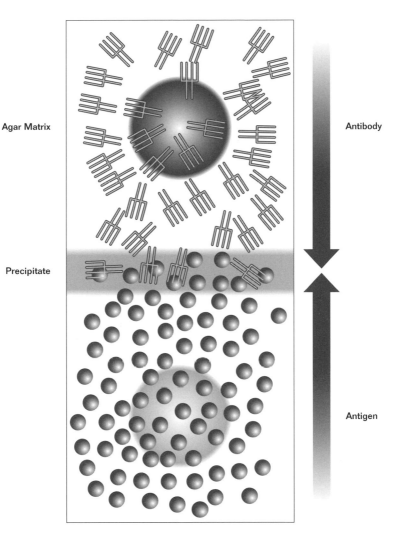

Above Precipitin test for human blood; if the substance is indeed human blood, a precipitin line forms where the antibodies meet the antigens as they diffuse along the gel plate.

near Osnabruck, where two young girls had vanished. The next day their bodies had been found, hacked to pieces, and local police had hunted for possible suspects. Their search turned up a jobbing carpenter named Ludwig Tessnow, who had been brought in for questioning as his clothing was heavily stained. On that occasion, too, he had claimed the stains were wood dye used in his work, and as a result he had been released and never charged. There was even a third case, involving animals rather than children. On June 11, a local farmer had found seven sheep disemboweled and hacked to pieces, but had seen a man running away from the scene at his approach. At a line-up he picked out Ludwig Tessnow as the man he had seen.

The Evidence

It was clear to Schmidt and to prosecutor Ernst Hubschmann that the only way to prove Tessnow was the killer was to disprove his claim that the stains on his clothing were wood dye. Then Schmidt learned that a biologist at Griefswald University, Professor Paul Uhlenhuth, had developed a reliable test for identifying bloodstains, which could even distinguish between human blood and animal blood, using serums from different animals to make the identifications. Items of Tessnow's clothing were confiscated and sent to the university laboratories for testing. The complex procedure took several days, but at the end the evidence was clear. On August 8, 1901, Uhlenhuth reported that he had tested more than a hundred dark spots showing on the clothing. He found there were indeed spots of wood dye on the overalls, and patches of sheep's blood on the jacket, but there were 17 distinct spots of human blood on his suit, shirt, overalls, and hat.

The Outcome

This proof that Tessnow's clothing was indeed stained with the blood of his victims was exactly what the prosecutors needed. He was put on trial for the murder of the young brothers, found guilty, and executed in Griefswald Prison in 1904, only a short distance away from the laboratory which had developed the tests that proved his guilt.

Hypochondriac Killer

Where: Dore, Sheffield, UK
When: October 23, 1983
Culprit: Arthur Hutchinson
Victims: the Laitner family
Cause of death: knife wounds
Forensic technique: serology

The Crime

Not all murders are carefully planned; some result from chance or
opportunity. The Laitner family lived in the upmarket Sheffield suburb of
Dore and were celebrating the marriage of their elder daughter in style on
October 23, 1983, with a marquee on the lawn. But the event was being
watched by a dangerous criminal from the cover of some nearby bushes. In
particular he was interested in Nicole Laitner, the 18-year-old sister of the
bride, but he was prepared to wait for the opportunity to gratify his desires.

Eventually the celebrations finished, the couple left on their honeymoon,
and the remainder of the family settled down for the night. The house was in
darkness when the intruder broke in through a patio door, and killed both
Nicole's parents and her brother with a series of knife attacks. He seized the
terrified girl, dragged her out to the wedding marquee, forced her to strip,
and then violently raped her. He then forced her back into her bedroom and
raped her twice more, before tying her up and vanishing into the night. She
escaped by first light and the search for the killer began.

The Case

After the frenzied stabbings, the inside of the house was awash with blood.
Most was clearly from the three murder victims, yet there were apparent
exceptions. There was blood on the girl's nightdress and on her bed
approximately at knee level, but she herself had not lost any blood. It seemed
this blood might have come from the attacker, who must have injured himself
somehow. Samples were sent to the Home Office Forensic Science Service at
Wetherby for analysis. A series of different factors—type, rhesus factor, and

the presence or absence of specific proteins or enzymes— identified one of the rarest of combinations, present in only 0.002 percent of the population, and this particular combination had already appeared in police records. A month before the Laitner killings, a woman had been raped in Selby. The suspect was a violent criminal named Arthur Hutchinson, who had previous convictions for theft and sexual assault. Unfortunately, he had escaped from custody on September 28 by jumping through a window and scrambling across a high wall topped with barbed wire. It was this that had cut his leg badly, and it seemed likely that this wound had opened up again when he attacked Nicole.

The Evidence
Tracking him down would have been extremely difficult, but for one significant failing of his, of which the police were aware. Hutchinson was a hypochondriac, who often visited hospital accident and emergency departments on the slightest pretext. In an attempt to trap him, a statement was issued that the barbed wire on top of the wall where he had escaped from custody had been given special treatment, and anyone who had come into close contact with it should seek medical attention, in case gangrene set in. He turned up at the Royal Infirmary in Doncaster, where he was treated for a gash to his knee, and police were able to arrest their prime suspect. After that, proving he was the killer was relatively straightforward. Not only did Nicole positively identify him as her attacker, but his shoes were matched to a footprint in the blood on the stairs at her family's house, and he had left a clear handprint on a bottle of champagne in the marquee. Finally, he had snacked while in the kitchen, and two pieces of cheese showed clear bite marks which were found to be a perfect match for Hutchinson's teeth.

The Outcome
Hutchinson was put on trial on September 4, 1984, and his defense collapsed after the prosecution introduced the watertight forensic evidence. After a ten-day trial he was found guilty of the rape and murders, and was jailed for life.

Dingo Attack

Where: Ayers Rock, Australia
When: August 17, 1970
Culprit: a dingo
Victim: Azaria Chamberlain
Cause of death: animal attack
Forensic technique: trace evidence

The Crime

In August 1980 Michael and Lindy Chamberlain took their two young sons, Aidan and Reagan, and their baby daughter Azaria on a camping holiday in Australia's remote interior. They set up their tent at a tourist site close to Ayers Rock, known to aboriginals as Uluru. On the evening of August 17, Azaria was asleep at the back of the tent with Reagan. Aidan was with his mother at the campsite barbecue where she was cooking supper, just 20 yards (18 m) from their tent. At around 8 PM, Michael heard a cry and Lindy rushed back to the tent. She saw a dingo emerge from the tent with something in its mouth which it was shaking furiously. She looked for the baby, but she was gone. The alarm was raised, search parties were sent out, but Azaria was never seen again.

The Case

On August 25, a tourist discovered some baby clothes, apparently neatly arranged, to the west of the rock. They were Azaria's, and showed traces of blood, though the jacket was missing. The clothes were checked for traces of dingo hair or saliva, but none were found. Reports indicated there were no tears in the clothing to suggest dingo bites, and investigators suggested the baby had been abducted and attacked, and her clothes left far from where she had been snatched. To back this up, they cited mistakes in the way the baby's clothes had been fastened and the presence of small adult handprints in the bloodstains. This leveled suspicion at the parents. Their car was searched and traces of blood spray were found on the carpet, around the seat supports, and on a pair of scissors in the vehicle. The Chamberlains were tried for the murder of their daughter in September 1982 and both were convicted.

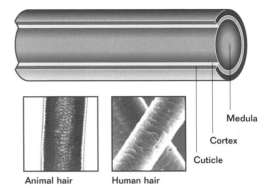

Right Animal hair is clearly distinguishable from human hair through differences in the root, pigmentation, scales and medualla.

Medula

Cortex

Cuticle

Animal hair   **Human hair**

The Evidence

The verdicts caused a furious reaction in Australia. Apart from sympathy for the parents, there were criticisms about restrictions placed on the defense and the standard of the evidence. For example the "blood spray" found in the car was later identified as a General Motors sound-deadening material, Dufix HN1081, sprayed under the car during manufacture which entered the interior through a hole in the wheel arch. The same pattern was found on other examples of that model, and in all cases showed positive in the tests for blood. Another test showed infant hemoglobin in the vehicle, but the Chamberlains lived in Mount Isa, which was a copper-mining district, where most everyday objects picked up microscopic copper deposits, which showed positive in the hemoglobin test. Finally, the damage to the baby's clothes was found to show ample evidence of bites, tears, and even dingo hairs, but this could only be checked two years after the trial.

The Outcome

Two appeals were rejected in spite of these conflicts. Only when Azaria's missing jacket was found more than five years later in a dingo's cave near the campsite, spattered with blood and badly torn, was Lindy's conviction reversed. She was released on February 7, 1986, and both she and Michael were finally cleared in September 1988. Since then there have been several dingo attacks on children of different ages, at least one of them fatal.

Martyrs or Murderers?

Where: South Braintree, Massachusetts, USA
When: April 15, 1920
Culprits: Nicola Sacco and Bartolomeo Vanzetti
Victims: Frederick Parmenter and Alessandro Beradelli
Cause of death: gunshot wounds
Forensic technique: ballistics

The Crime

Frederick Parmenter was paymaster of the Slater and Morrill Shoe Factories in the town of South Braintree in Massachusetts. On April 15, 1920 he was carrying more than $15,000 in payroll envelopes from one building to another some 200 yards (180 m) away, with security guard Alessandro Beradelli, when they passed two men dressed in dark clothing. One of them tried to grab Beradelli, but the other pulled out a gun and shot Parmenter twice and Beradelli five times, killing both men. A Buick sedan containing two other men pulled up and, joined by a lookout, all five piled the cash into the car and drove off at high speed. All that police found at the scene were spent cartridge cases of three different makes: Peters, Remington, and Winchester.

The Case

The getaway car was found in nearby woods. Police were able to link it to a failed robbery at another shoe factory in nearby Bridgewater, involving a criminal named Mike Boda. He owned this model of Buick, as well as an Overland, left for repairs at a garage in the village of Cochesett. The police asked the owners to phone them when Boda came to collect the car. On May 5 he arrived with a friend on a motorcycle and two more associates, named Sacco and Vanzetti, arrived on foot. By the time the police reached the scene, all four had left. Sacco and Vanzetti had caught the tram to Brockton. They were picked up at an intermediate stop, and searched. Both

Above Bullet casings from the Sacco and Vanzetti trial. The center line are the bullets removed from Berardelli's body.

men were armed: Sacco with a .32 Colt automatic and a pocket full of bullets, and Vanzetti with a .38 Harrington and Richardson revolver.

The Evidence

Both men appeared similar to eyewitness descriptions of the murder, but both denied any involvement and they did have convincing alibis. The crucial evidence was a .32 bullet found in Berardelli's body. The cartridges in Sacco's pocket were of the same type, and these were used for test firings to produce a comparison. When the test bullets were compared under a microscope with the one found in the victim's body, the minute scratches and scorings caused by the rifling in the barrel of the gun provided a perfect match.

Both men were convicted of murder and sentenced to death, but the case proved controversial from the outset. A self-proclaimed ballistics expert named Alexander Hamilton claimed the ballistics evidence was false, and a retrial was requested. Though his evidence at an earlier trial had nearly convicted an innocent man, Hamilton was allowed to make his case to the court. He brought in two Colt revolvers and dismantled them, together with Sacco's gun. It was only when he was caught trying to reassemble the barrel of the murder weapon on to one of his Colt pistols that the retrial was quashed. Later, Calvin Goddard of the Bureau of Forensic Ballistics in New York was able to demonstrate the closeness of the match between bullets which proved that the gun in Sacco's pocket had definitely killed the security guard.

The Outcome

Part of the problem was that Sacco and Vanzetti had no clear criminal connections, but they were known to be anarchists at a time when the authorities were worried by groups advocating a violent overthrow of society. Their supporters claimed that they were being executed for their political beliefs and many celebrities joined a campaign for their acquittal. They were executed on August 23, 1927, but in 1977 the Governor of Massachusetts issued what amounted to a proclamation of innocence. A team of forensic experts re-examined the evidence in 1961 and again in 1983. Both times the ballistics evidence was confirmed as accurate and true—what no one could prove was whether Sacco had been the person firing the gun on that fatal day.

Passion or Premeditation?

Where:	Corte Madera, California, USA
When:	February 27, 1991
Culprit:	James Mitchell
Victim:	Artie Mitchell
Cause of death:	gunshot wounds
Forensic technique:	ballistics

The Crime

James and Artie Mitchell were brothers who ran a successful business making pornographic films. Their productions were technically poor, entirely explicit, and cheap to make but they were also enormously lucrative. One reportedly cost $60,000 to make but earned $25 million. However, the brothers were having a succession of arguments which were becoming louder and more violent. By 1991, with Jim now aged 48 and Artie 46, their earnings and their differences reached their peak. At 10:15 PM on the night of February 27, Artie's girlfriend, Julie Bajo, called the police emergency line. Not only did she report a shooting, but the operator could clearly hear shots being fired, a fact later confirmed on the recording that is routinely made of all emergency calls.

The Case

When police turned up at Artie's house in Corte Madera, they found Jim Mitchell outside, apparently dazed by what had happened. He was holding a small-bore .22 rifle and had a .38 handgun in a shoulder holster, though this had not been fired. Inside they found the body of Artie lying in the bedroom and they found eight cartridge cases, although there were only three obvious bullet wounds—one in the abdomen, one in his right arm, and the third in his right eye. There was no need to prove that Jim Mitchell had fired the shots: ballistics evidence would have confirmed it, but he freely admitted having done so. But what had his motive been?

Those who knew the brothers well insisted that as the older brother, Jim had taken care of Artie throughout the years the two had been growing up and prospering in business together. Only the year before, Jim had risked his life by going into rough sea on a surfboard to save Artie and one of his sons who were in serious difficulties, and effectively saved them from drowning. So the most difficult question was, did the shooting of Artie Mitchell represent a case of premeditated murder or was it an all-consuming outburst of rage, which might make it a case of manslaughter?

The Evidence

The tape recording of the telephone conversation proved vital in trying to make a case for premeditated murder, since it established the time intervals between each of the shots. Though only five shots were heard, it was almost certain the first three had been fired before the call was connected and the recording began. Of the five on the recording, the most significant were shots three and four, which occurred with a gap of almost half a minute between them. The prosecution were trying to establish that this length of gap would have allowed someone suffering from anger time to reflect on what was happening, and to stop. To resume after this long an interval was, they said, clear evidence of premeditation and intent, hence the crime was murder. For the first time, crime scene experts used the evidence of where they had found the bullets to construct a three-dimensional computer-generated image of the shootings, ending with Artie being killed by the shot through his eye. This was seen by experts on the defense team as being a step too far, as it depended on too many assumptions over which shot was which in the sequence of sounds.

The Outcome

Jim Mitchell went on trial for his brother's murder 11 months after the shooting. His defense counsel undermined the prosecution reconstruction of the crime so effectively that the jury threw out the murder charge and on February 18, 1992 he was found guilty of manslaughter and sentenced to six years' imprisonment. After serving almost his entire sentence, including three years in San Quentin as a model prisoner, he was released on parole on October 3, 1997.

Part Four:

Naming the Victim

The Severed Arm

Where:	Sydney, Australia
When:	April 1935
Culprit:	unknown
Victim:	James Smith
Cause of death:	unknown
Forensic technique:	fingerprinting

The Crime

Two Australian fishermen donated a 10-foot (3-m) tiger shark, caught off the coast of Sydney, to the Coogee Beach Aquarium in April 1935. It began to show signs of increasing distress and then on April 25 it vomited up its stomach contents, which included a well-preserved human arm. Had this been a case of a shark attack on an innocent swimmer, or was this part of a dismembered body of a crime victim?

The Case

The limb was well muscled and remarkably well preserved, since it had been in the shark's stomach for some days without being digested. Experts concluded that this was due to the shark's reaction to the trauma of capture and confinement. As a result it was easy to see that the skin bore a tattoo showing two boxers confronting one another. A rope was tied around the wrist and there were clear signs that the arm had been hacked off its body by a knife rather than a shark bite. No other human remains were found in the shark's stomach, and so it was almost impossible to determine who the arm actually belonged to.

The Evidence

The only realistic hope was to find a way of retrieving the fingerprints. This involved removing the fragile layers of skin in pieces from the tip of each finger in turn and then carefully reassembling the fragments to produce a complete print. When complete, the prints were checked against criminal records and a match was found. The prints, and the arm, belonged to a former boxer and small-time criminal named James Smith who had already been reported missing. He had disappeared from home on April 8, telling his wife he was renting a cottage with a man named Patrick Brady (a known criminal) for the two men to do some fishing. A wide sea search failed to find any other parts of Smith's body, and closer expert examination revealed that the arm had been hacked off the body some time after death.

The Outcome

The killers have never been found, and the only motive appears to be inter-gang warfare in the Australian underworld— Patrick Brady was finally charged with Smith's murder, but the lack of solid evidence resulted in him being found not guilty.

Although Smith's murderer was never apprehended, through

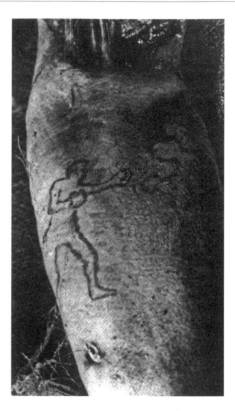

Above The tattooed arm of James Smith, disgorged by the captured tiger shark.

forensic techniques investigators had at least been able to identify the victim, even though only his arm was ever found, leaving one less unidentified body, and one less unsolved missing person case, in the criminal world.

The Jealous Doctor

Where:	Moffat, Scotland
When:	September 29, 1935
Culprit:	Dr. Buck Ruxton
Victims:	Isabella Ruxton and Mary Rogerson
Cause of death:	strangled
Forensic technique:	facial reconstruction

The Crime

On the morning of Sunday September 29, 1935, Susan Haines Johnson was walking over a stone bridge across a stream called the Gardenholme Linn, north of the small Scottish town of Moffat, when she happened to look down into the gully. There she saw a bundle out of which protruded a human arm. Over the following eight days the police investigation uncovered a succession of other body parts, including two heads, and later on two more bundles were found by the roadside in the area. All the badly decomposed fragments were taken to the Anatomy Department of the University of Edinburgh where they could be reassembled in a bid to establish their identities.

The Case

It was clear that cutting up the bodies so completely must have been a long and complex procedure as the culprit had gone to such lengths to obscure the victims' identities; fingerprints had been chopped off, the genitals had been removed, as had the facial skin along with ears, eyes, noses, and lips, and several teeth had been extracted. Such efforts would have required a detailed anatomical knowledge and must have taken around eight hours to complete. Investigators were able to establish when the parts had been dumped by the stream, as they were wrapped in newspaper dated September 15, two weeks before their discovery. In addition, a heavy rainstorm four days later would have washed away the bundles, so police began searching for people reported missing over that brief period. Eventually they found a newspaper report that the wife and maid of a Lancaster physician, Dr. Buck Ruxton, had both

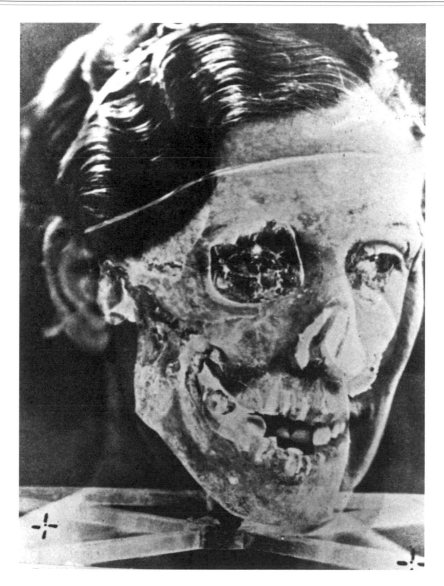

Above A portrait of Isabella Ruxton superimposed onto one of the skulls found at the scene.

vanished on September 14. After hearing reports of Ruxton's extreme jealousy toward his wife Isabella and his increasingly erratic behavior, police decided to search his house.

The Evidence

More evidence began to emerge: part of the newspaper wrapping turned out to be a particular edition of a national paper sold only in Morecambe and Lancaster, and a local news agent confirmed that a copy had been delivered to Ruxton's home on September 15. The head of one of the victims was wrapped in a set of child's clothing which had been passed on by the maid's mother for the Ruxtons' children. Finally, a search of the house revealed bloodstains and traces of human fat in the drains. On October 13, Ruxton was arrested for the murders of Isabella Ruxton and the maid Mary Rogerson. In the meantime, the bodies had been reconstructed as far as possible given the degree of mutilation, and both the height and the age fitted those of the missing victims.

Much more conclusive, though, was the information that was missing from the bodies, as numerous identifying marks and features had been removed in the dissection process: Mary had a squint and her eyes had been removed from her corpse; she had a birthmark on her arm and skin had been cut away from the site of the mark; an appendectomy scar had also been cut away as had a scar at the base of her thumb. Isabella's prominent teeth had been removed, as had her large nose. Then, through new and innovative forensic techniques, experts were able to superimpose a photograph on an image of her skull and found it a perfect fit. Finally, another expert studied the development of maggots in the body parts found on the riverbank and was able to show that both victims had died at about the time Isabella and Mary were last seen alive.

The Outcome

Dr. Ruxton was charged with both murders, and the overwhelming body of evidence convinced the jury, who found him guilty of both killings. He was executed on May 12, 1936. A confession released after his death claimed he had killed his wife in a fit of jealous rage, but the murder had been witnessed by the maid, who then became his second victim.

Acid Bath Murderer

Where:	Crawley, Sussex, UK
When:	February 1949
Culprit:	John George Haigh
Victim:	Olivia Durand-Deacon
Cause of death:	probable gunshot wound
Forensic technique:	bone analysis

The Crime

As a victim's body so often plays a crucial role in helping to identify their killer, some murderers try to escape detection and conviction by placing the bodies out of reach of investigators. John George Haigh was a successful and professional confidence trickster who charmed a succession of wealthy but lonely women into giving him money. Unfortunately, this created a disposal problem, since once he was successful, his lifestyle depended on being able to move on to find the next victim while at the same time evading arrest for his previous crimes. His solution was to kill his victims, and decided the best way to dispose of their remains was to dissolve each body in a bath of sulphuric acid, to destroy all evidence before it could be used against him.

The Case

The case that brought about his downfall began in February 1949 when Constance Lane and Haigh himself, both residents of the Onslow Court Hotel in South Kensington, London, reported that another resident, wealthy 69-year-old widow Olivia Durand-Deacon, had vanished. Haigh said that he had been due to meet her to discuss a business proposition at his workshop at Leopold Road, Crawley in Sussex, where he worked using strong acids to break down industrial materials, but claimed she had never arrived. When police interviewed hotel staff they discovered that Haigh owed money to the hotel and that he kept close company with several elderly and wealthy women. When they visited his workshop, they found containers of acid, a cleaner's receipt for a Persian lamb fur coat which belonged to Mrs. Durand-Deacon, and a recently fired Enfield revolver. Then, to their surprise, Haigh calmly admitted that they would never find the missing woman's body, as he had destroyed it with acid, leaving only a completely untraceable sludge. How could they prove murder with no body?

The Evidence

Intent on proving him wrong, the investigators returned to his workshop, and found large quantities of sludge in the yard outside. It contained a tiny pebble-like object that they were able to identify as a human gallstone, together with fragments of partly dissolved bones and a set of plastic dentures that was largely undamaged. The dentures were matched to those of the

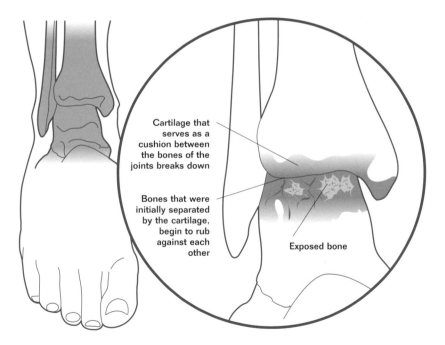

Cartilage that serves as a cushion between the bones of the joints breaks down

Bones that were initially separated by the cartilage, begin to rub against each other

Exposed bone

Above Investigators were aided in identifying the scanty remains of the victim due to the distinct signs of osteoarthritis that were evident in the recovered bone fragments.

victim after checking with her dentist. The bones were identified as human, from the spine, legs, and feet, and in addition the foot and ankle bones showed clear signs of severe osteoarthritis, a condition from which the victim had suffered, confirmed by Mrs. Durand-Deacon's family. Police also reconstructed the foot and took a plaster cast, which fitted one of the victim's shoes perfectly. Blood splashes on the wall of the workshop were consistent with the victim having been shot while she was bent over a bench, possibly studying business papers.

Other evidence found in the sludge included a strap from a handbag the victim was carrying on the day she disappeared, and the rest of the bag was later discovered hidden in the workshop yard. Experiments carried out with an amputated human foot and the body of a sheep showed, by the rate they were dissolved by concentrated sulphuric acid, that the body in the acid had been there since the day of the victim's disappearance. Other witnesses testified they had seen Haigh and the victim together on the afternoon she had vanished, though he returned alone to London that night.

The Outcome
The full story emerged step by step after the identification of the remains at the workshop. It seemed that Haigh, a chronic and unsuccessful gambler, was so short of cash that he had tried to interest his wealthy victim in a project to make and sell fake plastic fingernails. In the meantime, he bought large quantities of sulphuric acid and stored them at his workshop. On the day after Mrs. Durand-Deacon vanished he visited two jeweler's shops, one to sell her watch and the other to have items of her jewelry valued. Finally, when charged with her murder, Haigh admitted five other killings. He was put on trial and the jury proved so unimpressed by his assertion that without a victim's body he could not be convicted, that they took just 15 minutes to find him guilty of Mrs. Durand-Deacon's murder. He was hanged at Wandsworth prison on August 6, 1949.

Snowtown Monstrosities

Where:	Snowtown, Australia
When:	1993–99
Culprits:	James Vlassakis and 3 accomplices
Victims:	10 victims
Cause of death:	various
Forensic technique:	DNA matching

The Crime

Snowtown is a quiet little farming community some 90 miles (145 km) north of Adelaide in South Australia. Economic changes had resulted in several businesses closing down, leaving derelict buildings in the town, one of which was the local branch of the State Bank of South Australia. On May 20, 1999, a police squad from Adelaide visited the town as part of the closing stages of a year-long major operation, Operation Chart, a search for a group of three missing persons, one of whom had disappeared as early as 1993. They checked out the old bank building, and on opening the vault, their efforts were finally rewarded; they found an old couch, six large 44-gallon (200-liter) plastic barrels full of acid, as well as an array of knives, handcuffs, ropes, rubber gloves, and a device for generating electric shocks. And when they checked the contents of the barrels, they found they were full of body parts.

The Case

The three missing people who were the initial cause for the search were Clinton Douglas Tresize, missing since 1993, his friend Barry Wayne Lane, a transvestite pedophile, missing since October 1997, and Elizabeth Haydon, a 37-year-old mother of eight, missing since earlier that year. Lane was alleged to have had a ten-year affair with a man named Robert Wagner, one of a group of three men police suspected of being involved in the disappearances, along with Mark Haydon, husband of the missing Elizabeth, and John Bunting.

Local people had noticed the group visiting Snowtown, and when police were checking on the empty buildings in the town, they were told that the bank vault had been rented to a man supposedly using it for storing kangaroo carcasses. All three lived in the depressed northern suburbs of Adelaide, and were arrested on May 21. A fourth suspect, James Vlassakis, the 19-year-old son of Bunting's former girlfriend, was arrested two weeks later. When police searched Bunting's home they used ground-penetrating radar to find two more bodies, buried deep beneath the foundation of a rainwater tank.

The Evidence

When assembling the grisly evidence found in the old bank vault, investigators found they had fragments from eight different bodies, which, together with the ones dug up in Adelaide, made ten in all. Despite the effects of the acid, they managed to obtain fingerprints from some of the remains, but what also emerged from the investigation was a terrible tale of torture and mutilation. Some of the victims had been bound and gagged, some had feet and limbs hacked off, and others had suffered burns and electric shocks.

The most unexpected breakthrough in the case was the degree to which the victims' DNA had survived in bones, hair, and body tissues. Samples of this DNA were compared with that of relatives of the missing persons and one by one the victims were identified. An awful pattern was revealed: all the victims were known to the suspects as friends or neighbors, and in some cases were actually related to them. They had been murdered for their relatively meager welfare payments, or to use their identities to take out bank loans, and they had been tortured into signing documents, or even having their voices recorded on telephone answering machines to reassure family members worried at their disappearance.

The Outcome

When the quartet of suspects was brought to trial, Vlassakis admitted to murdering four of the victims, including his half-brother and stepbrother, and made an 800-page statement describing the role of the others. On September 9, 2003, the others joined him in receiving life sentences after a trial which had lasted 11 months in all.

Part Five:

Time of Death

Digesting the Evidence

Where:	Goderich, Ontario, Canada
When:	June 9, 1959
Culprit:	Steven Truscott
Victim:	Lynne Harper
Cause of death:	strangled
Forensic technique:	analysis of stomach contents

The Crime

On the evening of June 9, 1959, 14-year-old Steven Truscott was seen riding his sports bicycle along a lane leading away from the Royal Canadian Air Force base at Goderich, near Clinton in Ontario. Sitting on the crossbar was a schoolmate, 12-year-old Lynne Harper. Around 7 PM that same evening the pair were seen by another witness near a small copse called Lawson's Bush, though a third witness passing by the area a few minutes later reported that they had seen no sign of them there. Lynne was never seen alive again.

When she failed to return home that evening the alarm was raised, but it was not until two days later that her body was found, partly hidden by trees in Lawson's Bush. She was lying on her back, partly undressed, and strangled with her own blouse. Because of a continuing period of hot weather, her body had already begun to decompose, but a pair of footmarks found between her feet, which bore the imprint of crepe soles, suggested she had been raped, which investigators were able to confirm at her post-mortem. An analysis of her stomach contents showed a partly digested meal suggesting she had died before 7:30 PM at the latest, just thirty minutes after being seen with Steven Truscott.

The Case

When he was questioned by police, Steven Truscott said he had arrived home at 8:30 PM, an hour after Lynne's estimated time of death. He claimed to have dropped Lynne off at the nearby main road, where he had seen her get into a car, specifically a gray Chevrolet with US license plates. Since no one else had seen this car, and it did not accord with where she had been found or her time of death, no one believed his story.

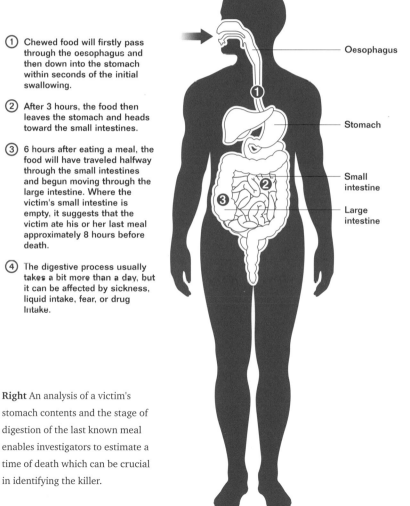

① Chewed food will firstly pass through the oesophagus and then down into the stomach within seconds of the initial swallowing.

② After 3 hours, the food then leaves the stomach and heads toward the small intestines.

③ 6 hours after eating a meal, the food will have traveled halfway through the small intestines and begun moving through the large intestine. Where the victim's small intestine is empty, it suggests that the victim ate his or her last meal approximately 8 hours before death.

④ The digestive process usually takes a bit more than a day, but it can be affected by sickness, liquid intake, fear, or drug intake.

Oesophagus

Stomach

Small intestine

Large intestine

Right An analysis of a victim's stomach contents and the stage of digestion of the last known meal enables investigators to estimate a time of death which can be crucial in identifying the killer.

The Evidence

Steven was arrested and given a medical examination. There were abrasions on his penis which suggested he had recently had sex with a degree of force, though he claimed these were the remains of a recent rash. He also had a graze on his left leg, his trousers were torn, and careful washing had failed to remove grass stains on the knees. Furthermore, he was known to have a pair of crepe-soled shoes, though these could no longer be found. Though the evidence was highly circumstantial, and lacked any definite proof that he had murdered Lynne, he was convicted and sentenced to death, though this was changed to life imprisonment on account of his age.

The Outcome

Because of the lack of solid evidence and his model behavior as a prisoner, Steven Truscott was granted leave to appeal against the sentence in 1967. The grounds for the appeal rested on different estimates of what the state of Lynne's stomach contents could reveal about her likely time of death. One school of thought was that the normal processes of digestion could be held up or stopped altogether by strong emotions or physical violence. This would render the relatively undigested meal almost irrelevant as an indicator of the time of death, which could have been at any time before her body was found in the two days which had elapsed since her disappearance. Had this been the case, it might have been possible that she was attacked and killed by the occupant of the mysterious Chevrolet and dumped at the copse not long before she was found, which would have put Steven Truscott out of the reckoning. Others disagreed, pointing out that the girl had been murdered at that spot, not merely brought back and dumped there. The appeal was denied, though two years later Steven Truscott was released on parole and went on to marry and raise a family under a completely new identity.

The Failed Alibi

Where:	Bloomington, Indiana, USA
When:	November 5, 1983
Culprit:	David Hendricks
Victims:	Hendricks' family
Cause of death:	hacked to death
Forensic technique:	analysis of stomach contents

The Crime

Businessman David Hendricks of Bloomington, Indiana, was often away from home, making frequent sales trips on behalf of his increasingly successful business, manufacturing orthopedic back braces. On Saturday November 5, 1983, while away on such a trip, he called home to speak to his wife and children. There was no reply to that call, nor to all the other calls he made during the course of the weekend, to his home and to friends and neighbors, so he finally called the local police and asked them to check the house. They did so at 10 PM on Tuesday November 8, as Hendricks was on his way home, and found Susan Hendricks and the three Hendricks children had all been hacked to death with an ax and a butcher's knife, both of which were still in the house, though they had been carefully wiped clean. Yet some signs did not quite fit the picture. A chest of drawers had been pushed over, but apart from that there was little disturbed apart from the victims' bodies, all of them in different rooms. The highly distressed David Hendricks was questioned about his trip, and he and his car were checked for traces of blood but none were found.

The Case

Hendricks' own explanation of the last time he had seen his wife and children seemed clear enough. On the Friday evening the family had gone out for dinner to a local pizza restaurant, where they had shared a family meal. They arrived at 6:30 PM, stayed an hour, and the children were home and in their beds by 9:30 PM. The parents had stayed up together until midnight, when

Susan retired to bed and David set off on his long drive to Wisconsin for the first customer call the next morning. On the face of it, he seemed entirely clear of the killings. Then he began to mention details of the crime which worried the police. They had deliberately not released much detailed information about the crime scene, but he began talking about burglars and various items being missing from the house, which he should have known nothing about. Was it possible he could have killed his family before he left, and then arranged for the police to check the house and find the bodies while he was still miles away on his business trip?

The Evidence

Post-mortems of the Hendricks children revealed a marked discrepancy over the times of their deaths. Hendricks had claimed all three were alive when he left at midnight, by which time the pizzas they had eaten at around 7 PM would have been mostly digested. In fact, the pizza toppings were still undigested, which suggested that the children had been killed even before 9:30 PM, the time Hendricks had claimed they had been put to bed. He then changed his departure time to 11:20 PM, which made no difference as the forensic evidence still discredited his version of events, and the contents of his wife's stomach confirmed she too was dead even before this earlier departure time.

The Outcome

Hendricks was put on trial for all three murders, and though the defense team tried to convince the jury that the time the children had spent playing energetically before going to bed would, like stress, have slowed down their digestive processes, this was not believed and Hendricks was found guilty of all three killings. On December 21, 1988, the sentences were upheld on appeal, but in 1991 a retrial was ordered and Hendricks was acquitted. More uncertainty had been cast on the reliability of stomach contents analysis in establishing the time of death, and the absence of other corroborative evidence left a degree of reasonable doubt.

Angel of Death

Where: Embu, Brazil
When: June 1985
Culprit: Dr. Josef Mengele
Victims: Auschwitz inmates
Cause of death: drowning
Forensic technique: forensic imaging

The Crime

Of all the horrors of the death camps operated by Hitler's Third Reich, few can equal the atrocities inflicted by "The Angel of Death," Dr. Josef Mengele. He carried out a series of sadistic experiments on his terrified victims, selected from among the inmates of the Auschwitz extermination camp. When the Nazi regime finally collapsed, Mengele fell into the Allies' hands, but amid the post-war chaos, he managed to escape to a new life in South America.

His family in Germany insisted he was dead, but there was a growing suspicion he may have survived, like so many other notorious missing Nazis, such as deputy Fuehrer Martin Bormann. Following the audacious Israeli capture of Adolf Eichmann, it was suggested that an official attempt be made to bring Mengele back to face justice too, but not until 1985 did the Americans announce an investigation to track him down. This was likely to be a difficult task in such a remote continent, especially as he would have spared no effort to invent a new identity in order to evade capture.

The Case

In the event, the task proved surprisingly easy, as the evidence found the investigators rather than the other way around. A German couple named Wolfram and Lieselotte Bossert claimed they knew where the now-dead Mengele was buried, and identified his grave as one bearing the name Wolfgang Gerhardt in the village of Embu in Brazil, where he had been buried at the age of 67 after a drowning accident in 1979. In June 1985 the grave was opened and a skeleton removed for examination by a range of experts from the United States and Germany.

The Evidence

Unfortunately, there was very little in the way of physical records relating to Mengele which could be used to verify the bones. His height was known to be 5 feet 8 inches (174 cm), and a dental chart from 1938 identified 12 fillings. The height of the skeleton, calculated from the bones of the leg and upper arm suggested a man around this height, and the dental chart showed a wider than usual space between two halves of the upper palate which accorded with his gap-toothed grin. Other tests were carried out: the shape of the pelvis suggested it was male, the shape of the nose and eye sockets suggested a

Above Forensic team presenting evidence identifying the exhumed skeleton as that of Dr. Mengele.

Caucasian, and the amount of abrasion of the teeth suggested a subject who had been between 60 and 70 years old at death. But while all this evidence did not rule out the possibility the corpse was Mengele, it did not positively confirm it either. A major step forward was achieved by German forensic anthropologist Richard Helmer, who made a series of high-resolution video images of the skull, allowing photographs of Mengele to be superimposed on the appropriate image, so that individual features of the skull could be compared. The correlation between photos and video images was close enough for it to be highly probable that this was indeed Mengele's corpse.

The Outcome

Final confirmation had to wait until 1992, when DNA samples from Mengele's known living relatives in Germany were compared with samples produced from the skeleton exhumed from the grave. When the match was confirmed as positive, the Angel of Death was laid to rest at last.

Predicting the Progress of Time

Where: New Jersey, USA
When: November 1971
Culprit: John List
Victims: List's family
Cause of death: gunshot wounds
Forensic technique: forensic anthropolgy

The Crime

Recent forensic science developments, such as the reconstruction of facial features from skulls of long-dead victims or retrieving DNA samples from skeletal remains, have brought killers to justice after years, or even decades, have passed since their crime was committed. For example, New Jersey accountant John List, who vanished after killing his wife, their three teenage children, and his mother in November 1971, was captured and charged with his crimes after 18 years of freedom.

The Case

The murders were discovered on December 7, 1971, when police went to investigate why lights were ablaze in the Lists' large Victorian house, "Breeze Knoll," for night after night even though they were away on vacation. In the mansion's large ballroom they found the bodies of Helen List, the couple's daughter, and two sons, each one neatly laid out on a sleeping bag and all suffering gunshot wounds. In the small upstairs apartment was the corpse of List's own mother, Alma, who had also been shot. Of List himself there was no sign. He had left letters that explained he had killed his family to protect their souls from corruption by the world's increasing moral breakdown. His car was found in a JFK airport parking lot but there the trail ended. As the years passed, it seemed he had escaped justice.

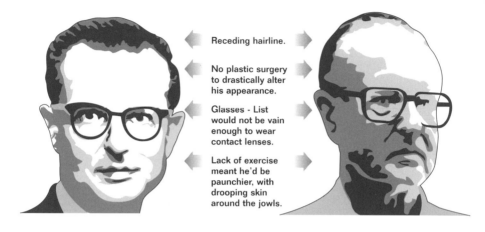

Receding hairline.

No plastic surgery to drastically alter his appearance.

Glasses - List would not be vain enough to wear contact lenses.

Lack of exercise meant he'd be paunchier, with drooping skin around the jowls.

Above The forensic artist produced an accurate likeness of John List 18 years after the murder, based on his habits and lifestyle, predicitng how age would have affected his features.

The Evidence

After his dramatic escape, a vast amount of publicity featured List's picture, but no helpful sightings resulted. The only person who thought she might have seen him was a Wanda Flannery, living in Aurora, Colorado. She read an article on the murders in *Weekly World News* magazine in February 1987, and noticed that John List closely resembled one of her neighbors named Robert Clark, who lived with his second wife Delores. She spoke to Delores about the resemblance, but her angry rebuttal calmed Ms. Flannery's suspicions and the matter was dropped. In the following year, the Clarks moved to a new home in Richmond, Virginia.

In the meantime, Captain Frank Marranca who had been appointed head of the Major Crimes Unit in Elizabeth, New Jersey, approached the producers of a popular TV series on cold cases, *America's Most Wanted*, which had proved successful in tracking down several criminal fugitives. As the producers were concerned at the lack of a recent picture of John List, forensic sculptor Frank Bender was called in to produce a likeness of how List might look after 18 years. This time, they would not be working from a skull, but with a computer program that had been devised to simulate the effects of aging. An expert criminal profiler, Dr. Richard Walter, was asked to assess the effects of List's attitudes and lifestyle to determine how his appearance would have changed over the years, and advise the computer specialists which factors to use in running the program.

He decided List's religious background would rule out radical plastic surgery, that his avoidance of exercise would cause him to put on weight, and that his need for spectacles would have developed into having to use larger and thicker glasses as he grew older. All these factors were used in generating a new image for the basis for a sculpture, which was used in the televised reconstruction of the crimes broadcast on May 21, 1989. Ironically, John List normally watched the show, but missed that edition as he and Delores were at a church social. But Wanda Flannery did not.

The Outcome

More than 300 phone calls resulted from the TV program. The one that finally brought an end to List's escape was from Wanda Flannery's son-in-law who gave them the Clarks' new address in Richmond, Virginia. Two FBI agents checked out the lead, and Robert Clark was arrested and finally put on trial under his original identity for the murders of his family. After a seven-day trial he was found guilty on April 12, 1990 and given five life sentences.

The Last of the Romanovs

Where:	Ekaterinburg, Russia
When:	July 17, 1918
Culprit:	Communist regime
Victims:	Russian Imperial family
Cause of death:	gunshot wounds
Forensic technique:	DNA matching

The Crime

After the Bolshevik Revolution, Nicholas II, the last Tsar of Russia, and his family were moved under heavy guard to imprisonment at the Ipatiev House in Ekaterinburg in the Urals. Orders came from Moscow that they were to be executed, and at 2 AM on July 17, 1918 they were lined up in the cellar of the house and shot, together with their physician, a maid, and two male servants. What happened to their bodies after that remained a mystery for decades.

The Case

Sixty years later, an Interior Ministry film producer named Gely Ryabov made contact with the family of a guard, Yakov Yurovsky, who had seen the murders carried out. Ryabov discovered that the victims had initially been taken to a mineshaft called the Four Brothers, then moved over a long-abandoned cart track called the Koptyaki Road to a field north of the town where they were buried in boggy ground. With the help of local experts, Ryabov traced the route taken by the truck and on the burial site they found a layer of logs covering a pile of bones and fragments of quality clothing. The bones were stored in the Ekaterinburg morgue, and in 1991 Russian President, Boris Yeltsin, ordered an official enquiry to determine their identities.

The Evidence

Though the two largest skulls seemed to match photographs of the Tsar and Tsarina, this fell short of solid proof. DNA evidence was difficult as the bones had deteriorated badly over the years. However, initial DNA analysis at the Home Office Forensic Science laboratories in the UK showed that five of the nine skeletons found were at least from the same family. Confirming who that family was would depend on establishing a link with surviving relatives through mitochondrial DNA, passed on through female ancestors. Samples were collected by exhuming dead members of the family and by contacting living relations abroad. For the Tsarina and the children, links were tested by a DNA sample from Prince Philip, Duke of Edinburgh, related to the family through his grandmother Victoria, Marchioness of Milford Haven, who was the Tsarina's elder sister. In all, the process of identification took seven years of painstaking testing, but at the end of January 1998 chief investigator Vladimir Solovyov announced that five skeletons were from the ruling family. Measurements of the bones established they were the Tsar and Tsarina, and their daughters Olga, Tatiana, and Anastasia. The remains of the heir to the throne, Alexei, and the Grand Duchess Maria, were missing.

The Outcome

After the identification, a tug-of-war began over the remains. Ekaterinburg wanted them buried in a new cathedral built on the site of Ipatiev House, and Moscow wanted them for its new cathedral. Finally, President Yeltsin, who had originally given the orders for the destruction of the Ipatiev House in 1977 when serving as party boss in the area, insisted they be interred in the Imperial family vault in the St. Peter and St. Paul Cathedral in St. Petersburg. On July 17, 1998, the 80th anniversary of the execution, the Tsar and his family were at last given a state funeral and reburial.

Right Portrait of the Russian Imperial family, 1913.

Part Six:

Bites, Knives, and Profiles

Trail of a Serial Killer

Where:	USA
When:	1969–78
Culprit:	Ted Bundy
Victims:	between 40 to 50 victims
Cause of death:	various
Forensic technique:	criminalistics

The Crime

Sometimes a killer may be smart enough, or lucky enough, to evade detection for several killings in succession. But as a serial killer's confidence grows and the evidence from their numerous crimes accumulates, it often results in the criminal being identified, and tied to at least one of the crimes they committed. Ted Bundy was one of the most prolific of America's serial killers, carrying out a series of murders of young women over a nine-year period across a huge swath of the continental United States. He began killing in California in 1969, moved north into Oregon and Washington, and then headed east into Colorado and Utah. Surprisingly, he was identified on several occasions as present in the area where murders took place, but there was no specific evidence to prove his guilt. Even when he finally did make a mistake, and was jailed for the attempted killing of another young woman, he managed to escape and subsequently resumed his violent and grisly career.

The Case

Ted Bundy's first mistake leading to his capture was made in November 1974 when he reached Salt Lake City. Pretending to be a plainclothes police officer, he ordered 18-year-old Carol DaRonch to get into his VW Beetle to go to the parking lot where someone had been seen trying to break into her car. He was plausible enough at first, but when he tried to handcuff her and then, whenn that failed, to hit her with a crowbar concealed in the vehicle, she managed to escape. Police began watching for VW Beetles, although these were extremely common on the roads of the USA. Finally, on August 16, 1975, a Salt Lake City police officer pulled up a Beetle to check the driver's papers. Inside was

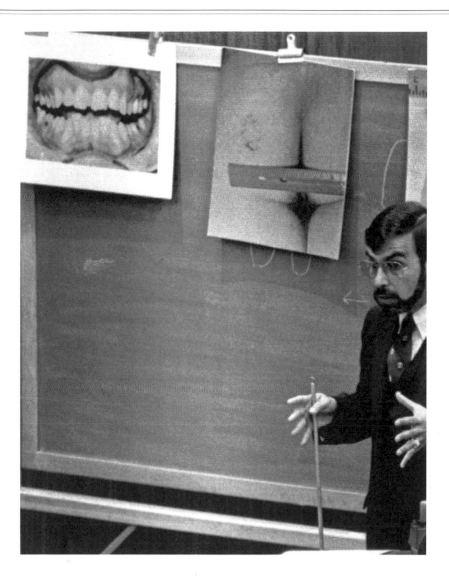

Above Dr. Levine, a forensic odontologist, testifies at Bundy's trial that the bite marks found on the buttock of victim Lisa Levy reflect characteristics of Bundy's teeth.

Ted Bundy, together with the crowbar and the pair of handcuffs. He was tried and sentenced to 15 years in jail for attempted murder.

Meanwhile, police were collecting more and more evidence from earlier murders which pointed in Bundy's direction. But before additional charges could be brought in the summer of 1977, he had escaped from custody and been recaptured, only to escape again six months later. This time he moved to Florida where the killings began again.

On one evening in January 1978, Bundy attacked five women on the Tallahassee campus of Florida State University, leaving two dead, two seriously injured by vicious head blows, and another well enough to identify him. He was finally recaptured in Pensacola after he had killed one final victim, a 12-year-old girl named Kimberly Leach.

The Evidence

By the time Leach's body was found it had decomposed too badly to provide much direct evidence, although bloodstains and semen traces on her underwear were of the same type as Bundy's and prints identical to the soles of his shoes were found next to the body. But the evidence which had most effect on the jury at his trial would be a series of bite marks on the breast and buttocks of one of his Tallahassee victims, Lisa Levy. Odontologist Dr. Richard Souviron showed them photographs of Bundy's teeth and compared the unusual features with the bite marks, to convince them that the match was a perfect one.

The Outcome

Ted Bundy's trial began on June 25, 1979 in Miami for the Florida University murders. On July 23 he was found guilty of both killings and sentenced a week later to the electric chair. He was also charged with the murder of Kimberly Leach early the following year, and was again given a death sentence. A series of appeals over ten years proved unsuccessful, and he was finally executed on January 24, 1989 at Raiford State Penitentiary, having confessed beforehand to between 40 and 50 murders.

The Jagged Tooth

Where: Biggar, Scotland
When: August 6, 1967
Culprit: Gordon Hay
Victim: Linda Peacock
Cause of death: strangled
Forensic technique: odontology

The Crime

On August 6, 1967, 15-year-old schoolgirl Linda Peacock went missing from her home in the small Scottish town of Biggar, some 25 miles (40 km) south-west of the city of Edinburgh. At around 10 PM on the night of her disappearance, witnesses had seen a girl matching her description standing by the cemetery gates in town, talking to a young man, and another witness reported hearing a scream around 20 minutes later. Early the following morning, her body was found inside the churchyard. She had been badly beaten and finally strangled with a rope.

The Case

When her body was examined, it was clear her killer had not raped her, although her clothes were disturbed and there was a prominent oval bruise on her right breast. Closer inspection showed this was actually a bite mark, and it was carefully photographed. Because there were unusual features about the bite, investigators decided to call in forensic dentistry expert Dr. Warren Harvey, who confirmed that the specific characteristics of the mark could help identify the killer.

The Evidence

The police had checked almost the whole population of the small town and the surrounding area, a total of more than 3,000 people, with no success at all. The only group of people still left unchecked were the 29 inmates of a juvenile detention center in the town, and Dr. Harvey decided this was a small enough group to make dental comparisons viable. The key feature of the bite mark was one unusually jagged tooth, and when all the inmates had been asked to provide a bite impression for comparison purposes, there were five where the resemblance to the bite on Linda's body was close enough to cause suspicion. One in particular was 17-year-old Gordon Hay, who had been arrested and was serving time in the center for breaking into a factory. He had told other inmates the night before her disappearance that he had met Linda at the local fair, and that he wanted to have sex with her. On the night she vanished, he was found missing from the detention center, and was seen on his return to be out of breath, disheveled, and covered in mud.

The Outcome

Unmasking Hay as the killer depended on producing a more exact match between his teeth and the bite mark. Dr. Harvey took another more precise impression and noticed evidence of sharp-edged pits in the tips of the upper and lower right canine teeth, the result of a rare condition called hypocalcination. This in itself was highly unusual. In Hay's case, the pit in the upper tooth was lower than that in the lower canine, which when combined with the site of the pits made a perfect match with the bite mark, almost as conclusive as a fingerprint. To back up the diagnosis, Dr. Harvey examined the teeth of 342 young soldiers of similar age to Hay, and found only two with pitted teeth, one with a pit and hypocalcination. None had two pits and hypocalcination. Though the defense lawyers tried hard to discredit the dental evidence, when considered together with the witness statements on his absence the night of the girl's murder and his condition on his return, it was enough to result in a guilty verdict.

Conflicting Evidence

Where: Fort Bragg, North
                     Carolina, USA
When: February 17, 1970
Culprit: Jeffrey MacDonald
Victims: MacDonald's family
Cause of death: knife wounds
Forensic technique: criminalistics

The Crime
Forensic evidence must be assessed with complete impartiality. In murder charges against former US Army officer Jeffrey MacDonald, the case remains controversial because of claims that defense evidence was lost or suppressed. MacDonald served as an Army doctor assigned to Special Forces units at Fort Bragg in North Carolina, and was married with two young daughters. On the cold, showery night of February 17, 1970 military police at the post rushed to the family home after MacDonald called them. They found his wife and daughters dead from multiple stab wounds, while Jeffrey MacDonald was apparently unconscious and had to be given mouth-to-mouth resuscitation.

The Case
Afterward he claimed he had been roused from sleep on the living-room sofa by the screams of his wife and their older daughter. Three men were standing over him: two white men and a black man wearing staff-sergeant's stripes. They were armed with a large knife, an ice pick, and a baseball bat, and behind them stood a woman with long blond hair in a floppy hat. He was set upon, stabbed and beaten, but was able to partly defend himself by wrapping his pajama jacket around his hands, and finally his attackers fled. He tried and failed to revive his family, but investigators were suspicious. How was MacDonald able to describe his attackers in detail when the room was in darkness and his vision was extremely poor without spectacles?

The Evidence

The forensic evidence triggered further doubts. Fibers from his pajama jacket were found under his wife's body and trapped beneath the fingernails of one of his daughters, though there were none in the living room where he had struggled with his attackers and where there was little sign of disarray. Splashes of his blood were found in the kitchen, bathroom, and on a pair of spectacles, but not in the living room or on the phone used to call the police. His pajama jacket was analyzed in the FBI labs, but the pattern of cuts was not consistent with an attack, and suggested instead an attempt to stage the murder scene. Furthermore, no traces of any intruders were found to support his story.

On the other hand, the defense team still insists that a colonel's daughter, Helena Stoeckley, who was a member of a drug trafficking ring, had been seen making her way to the MacDonald house on the night of the murder wearing a floppy hat and a long, blond wig, and that hairs from that wig found at the murder scene were disallowed as evidence. Fragments of human skin found under the fingernail of Mrs. MacDonald, which were not from her husband, were lost, and hairs and fibers that did not belong to the household were either mislaid or suppressed as evidence. Finally a bloody palm print was found on the footboard of Mrs. MacDonald's bed, and was not identified as belonging to any of the family.

The Outcome

At first the Army charged Jeffrey MacDonald with the murders but the charges were dropped and he was given an honorable discharge from the service at the end of the year, and started working in a California hospital. After complex legal maneuvers, he was again charged with the murders and finally convicted on August 29, 1979. Because of legal errors, he was then released a year later to return to his job, only to be rearrested again and imprisoned in March 1982. Since then, there have been a succession of appeals and applications, but MacDonald remains in prison. Meanwhile, Helena Stoeckley died in January 1983, but in April 2007 her mother, living in a Fayettville nursing home, revealed her daughter had told her that MacDonald was innocent, and that she herself had broken into the family home with three men responsible for the killings.

The Road Rage Murder

Where:	Bromsgrove, West Midlands, UK
When:	December 1, 1996
Culprit:	Tracie Andrews
Victim:	Lee Harvey
Cause of death:	knife wounds
Forensic technique:	criminalistics

The Crime

The pressures of driving on increasingly congested roads have spawned the frighteningly familiar condition of "road rage." Lee Harvey and his girlfriend Tracie Andrews, a young couple returning home from an evening in a pub at Bromsgrove in the West Midlands on December 1, 1996 appeared to have been victims of just such an explosion of aggression. At around 11 PM, they overtook a dark-colored Ford Sierra containing two or three men. The other driver then accelerated and tailgated their Escort Turbo, flashing his headlights. Harvey turned off the main road but the other car managed to pull in front and forced the couple to stop. Harvey got out to confront the other driver, but was subjected to a frenzied knife attack and was left bleeding profusely from more than 30 wounds in the arms of his girlfriend, who had been hit in the face by one of their attackers. The other vehicle sped off and the emergency services were called, but Harvey died without regaining consciousness.

The Case

After a huge search to try to find the other car and its occupants, described in some detail by Andrews, police became worried by unexplained gaps appearing in her story. One witness, Susan Duncan, a retired detective constable who lived in the area and had arrived on the scene just after the attack, said she had not heard another vehicle driving away from the scene, and this was corroborated by other local witnesses.

By this time more and more people were revealing the constant fights between the couple; one witness had seen them in the bar on the evening of the murder behaving angrily toward one another, while the police records showed that after complaints by Andrews they had intervened on one occasion. It also emerged that while in hospital Andrews had made half a dozen visits to the toilets before she was searched and interviewed, arousing suspicions that she might have been trying to dispose of evidence.

The Evidence

By the time suspicions had been aroused, it was too late to retrieve whatever might have been dumped in the toilets; the bin for clinical waste and hand towels, a perfect hiding place, had already been

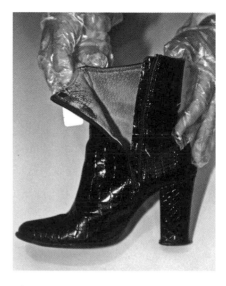

Above Andrews' bloodstained boot where detectives believe she kept the knife.

emptied. However, a thorough search of the murder scene uncovered a tiny spring and a pair of tweezers, identified as part of an imitation Swiss Army knife. The autopsy showed that this type of knife could certainly have produced the wounds suffered by Harvey. The knife was not found, but an examination of Andrews showed a complex blood pattern inside the top of her boot which corresponded with the blade of such a knife, and she could have hidden it there until she was able to dispose of it. A close examination of the blood patterns on her clothing also showed inconsistencies with her explanation of how close she had been to Harvey when he was attacked.

The Outcome

Six months later, Andrews was charged with Harvey's murder. She was found guilty and sentenced to life imprisonment. She announced her intention to appeal against her conviction, but this was disallowed, and she later confessed to the crime while in prison.

Mad Bomber of New York

Where: New York, USA
When: 1940–56
Culprit: George Metesky
Victims: no fatalities
Cause of death: homemade bombs
Forensic technique: criminal profiling

The Crime

Between the early 1940s and the mid-1950s, New York City suffered a series
of incidents involving homemade bombs, though several of these failed to
explode. There was a period during World War II and beyond when they
seemed to have stopped, but the bombs reappeared in 1950 and became
more threatening as more and more detonated successfully. Eventually a
device that was left in a crowded Brooklyn cinema in December 1956 injured
several people. It was clear that unless police caught the person behind the
campaign, it would not be long before innocent victims were killed.

The Case

The only link to the person behind the bombs was a series of notes, which
were either left with the bombs or sent directly to the police. Sometimes these
would be handwritten, on other occasions they were assembled from letters
cut out of newspaper headlines. The first bomb was placed outside the offices
of the Consolidated Edison power company in central Manhattan on
November 16, 1940 with a note that simply said "CON EDISON
CROOKS, THIS IS FOR YOU." Another was left at the same location a
year later before the wartime interruption to the campaign, and when the
bombs resumed in 1950, the letters also continued, but they still seemed to
contain no clue that would lead police to the person behind them.

In desperation, the New York police contacted Dr. James Brussel, a
criminal psychiatrist working in the city, for advice as to the kind of person
they should be looking for. To their amazement and skepticism, he told them
the person responsible was a middle-aged, heavily built Roman Catholic

male, born overseas and living with a brother or sister, probably in the state of Connecticut to the east of the city. He would be unmarried and probably suffering from paranoia, with a deep hatred for his father and an obsessive love for his late mother. They would probably find him wearing a double-breasted suit with the jacket buttoned up, and he was likely to have worked for Consolidated Edison at some point in his life.

The Evidence

Dr. Brussel was able to draw these conclusions based on the evidence in the notes. The phrases used suggested that the writer felt he lived in a hostile world, hinting at paranoia. This condition normally peaks when a person is around 35 years old, which, over the 16 years since the first of the bombs appeared, would now put him in his early 50s, a conjecture supported by the care taken in printing the letters and assembling the increasingly sophisticated bombs. Quirks in the language used in the notes suggested someone who was not a native English speaker, but the grammar was correct, indicating a successfully completed high school education. At the time, using bombs as weapons was most associated with Slavic ethnic groups, predominantly those of a Catholic background, while the sites where the letters had been posted pointed toward someone who traveled between the city and the commuter belt of Connecticut.

Other more subtle clues suggested the writer suffered from an Oedipus complex, usually associated with losing one's mother while young and developing a hatred for the father, as well as a tendency to find refuge in living with a sibling. Finally, double-breasted suits were reasonably fashionable at the time, and buttoning up the jacket would be a predictable defense against the outside world for someone with these problems.

The Outcome

This was an astonishing piece of profiling, but failed to lead the police to identifying the bomber. Dr. Brussel suggested releasing the detailed description to the papers, which produced a phone call from the bomber, showing they had hit the target. In the meantime the police checked records of everyone working for the Consolidated Edison group who might have

Roman Catholic male

Obsessive love for
his late mother

Deep hatred for
his father

Living with a
brother or sister

Heavily-built male

Wears
double-breasted
suit buttoned up

Left Through subtle
clues in his actions and
notes, the criminal
profiler on the case was
able to provide some
astonishingly accurate
details about the Mad
Bomber of New York.

suffered accidents or other mishaps.
They finally found the name of
George Metesky, with an address in
Waterbury, Connecticut, who had
been injured on the same date as a
reference given in one of the notes.
The company had kept a series of
letters from Metesky when he had
been pursuing an unsuccessful
claim for compensation, in which he had threatened retribution and used the
phrase "dastardly deeds," words which had also appeared in one of the notes.

Police called at his address to arrest him, and found him wearing a
dressing gown. To go to the police station, he changed into a double-breasted
suit and buttoned up the jacket. He was tried and found guilty but insane,
and confined in an asylum until his release in 1973. He then returned to his
family and the house in Waterbury where he lived until his death in 1994, at
the age of 90.

The Railway Rapist

Where:	London, UK
When:	1982–86
Culprit:	John Patrick Duffy
Victims:	numerous
Cause of death:	strangled
Forensic technique:	criminal profiling

The Crime

No matter how carefully a serial criminal may plan and carry out his or her crimes to evade detection, they still unsuspectingly reveal patterns in their misdeeds which lead investigators closer to their quarry. Criminal profilers study these patterns and can use them to narrow down the search to simplify the task of the investigators.

The case of the so-called "Railway Rapist," who attacked a series of victims in London and the surrounding suburbs between 1982 and 1986, was one of the first where profiling helped solve the case. In the first assaults, the attacker followed a pattern of first talking to a potential victim to lull suspicion before suddenly producing a knife. He would then tie her hands and subject her to a violent rape.

The Case

His victims described him as around 5 feet 9 inches (175 cm) tall, fair-haired with piercing eyes, and aged between 25 and 30, but all were unable to supply sufficient detail that could identify a specific individual. Then the rapist started to murder his victims, strangling them with a tourniquet after the attack. He took care to destroy evidence, wiping away all traces of the rapes on those he left alive and burning the pubic areas of those he killed to destroy any potential trace evidence.

The Evidence

Additional patterns in the crimes soon emerged. Locations for the earlier attacks and sites where the bodies of later victims were found were close to the rail network around suburban London. The first rapes occurred around Kilburn in north-west London, suggesting this was close to the attacker's home at that point, and the timings of the attacks showed that his job must have been one with flexible hours to allow time to carry out the attacks.

The profiler, Professor David Canter of Sussex University, also concluded that his easy conversations with female victims showed he was probably married or in a long-term relationship, and the fact that he had raped and killed a 15-year-old victim, Maartje Tamboezer, implied he probably had no children of his own. Professor Canter also suggested the rapist's job involved little public contact, that he would not have had more than one or two close male friends, and little contact with women other than his immediate partner,

The profile seemed a close fit with the 1505th name on the police list of 2,000 potential suspects. John Patrick Duffy was living near Kilburn, and had been arrested for raping his former wife after their separation. He worked as a railway carpenter, allowing him time off during the working day, and explaining his familiarity with the network. Also, tourniquets were used in emergency treatments for accidents with sharp carpenter's tools.

The Outcome

When he was arrested, police found fibers from the sheepskin coat worn by one of the victims on items of Duffy's clothing. They also found samples of the unusually wide type of string used to bind his victims, and the surviving victims all identified him as their attacker. He was tried for the rapes and murders, and sentenced to life imprisonment on February 26, 1988. One of the details in the profile—having one or two close male friends—was corroborated by his having an accomplice in the first rapes. David Mulcahy, a friend of Duffy's from childhood, was charged in 1999 with being an accessory to several rapes and one of the murders and also given a life sentence.

It emerged that when appearing in court following the attack on his ex-wife, Duffy had seen one of his earlier victims, who looked right at him though clearly failed to recognize him. It seemed likely that from that point onward he decided to kill his victims so that the danger of being identified was eliminated. In prison he admitted to having committed 17 more rapes and one murder in addition to those with which he had been charged.

Part Seven:
Forgery and Impersonation

Defrauding a Recluse

Where: New York, USA
When: 1970–72
Culprit: Clifford Irving
Crime: fraud
Forensic technique: handwriting and voice
                     analyses

The Crime

By the 1970s American tycoon and aviation pioneer Howard Hughes had
become increasingly eccentric and retired from his high-security Las Vegas
hotel to a refuge in the Bahamas, severing all contact with outsiders. Given
his place in twentieth-century history, any authorized biography was bound
to command vast sums on the open market. So when Clifford Irving, a
moderately successful author, claimed Hughes had agreed he should write the
biography from a series of interviews, publishers reacted with suspicion. They
could not contact Hughes for confirmation, but Irving produced documents
signed by the recluse permitting the book to appear on payment of $765,000
to a Swiss bank account in Hughes' name. They were declared genuine by
Osborn, Osborn, and Osborn, experts in document authentication, and
publishers McGraw-Hill paid the advance and commissioned Irving to go ahead.

The Case

All went well until the announcement that the Time-Life magazine group had
bought the serial rights to the now completed manuscript. This produced a
phone call to the group's offices from the Hughes Tool Company to set up
conference call facilities for an interview between reporters and Hughes
himself. Reporters fired questions at the person claiming to be Hughes for 20
minutes, concentrating on personal details to prove his identity. The answers
were accurate—one involved the cockpit design of an aircraft produced by
Hughes, another the piece of chewing gum stuck to the tail of one of his
record attempt aircraft for good luck. During this call Hughes declared that
he had never met Irving, had never given him permission to produce a

biography, and had never received any advance payment.

The Evidence

Irving then produced letters from Hughes and drafts of the book with Hughes' own amendments written on the margins. These were shown to a specialist document examiner for the US Postal Service, along

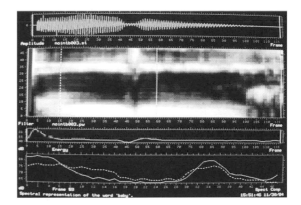

Above Computer graphics screen image of waveform representations of a voiceprint.

with samples of Irving's handwriting. After a detailed analysis, he agreed there was a close resemblance with Hughes' handwriting, but decided the documents were high-quality fakes, and showed similarities with Irving's own hand.

There still remained the identity of the voice in the media interview. Comparison was made between a recording of a speech by Hughes to a 1947 Senate hearing, and the interview recordings. The results were studied by two experts—Lawrence Kersta who had produced the first voice prints (graphic analyses of an person's voice which are as individual as fingerprints) at the Bell Telephone laboratories in 1963, and Dr. Peter Ladefoged, Professor of Phonetics at UCLA. Bearing in mind the age difference between the recordings, both men insisted the voice was that of Howard Hughes on both occasions.

The Outcome

The missing advance payment was traced to an account at the bank to which the cheque had been sent, opened by Irving's wife under the name Helga R. Hughes. As the advance cheque was made out to H. R. Hughes, she had been able to transfer the payment into her own account. Both Irving and his wife were tried for fraud and in June 1972 they were found guilty and sent to jail—Irving for two and a half years and his wife for 18 months.

The Hitler Diaries

Where:	Germany
When:	February 1981
Culprits:	Konrad Kujau and Gerd Heidemann
Crime:	forgery
Forensic technique:	document analysis

The Crime

For years after the end of World War II, historians speculated about the lack of any form of personal diary kept by Adolf Hitler, which could throw new light on the events of the war and the rise of the Nazis. The likely explanation was that any such diaries had been destroyed as the Third Reich tottered to defeat in 1945. However, in February 1981, Gerd Heidemann, a journalist on the West German current affairs magazine *Stern*, was shown a pile of 27 bound volumes of handwritten text produced by a document collector who had lived in Communist East Germany. These, he claimed, were the missing diaries, written in Hitler's own hand, hidden since the plane flying them out of Berlin had crashed in the east of the country. He was now offering them, along with an unsuspected third volume of Hitler's book *Mein Kampf*, to the publishers of the magazine, Gruner and Jahr, for the equivalent of $2 million.

The Case

The publishers put up the money and took delivery of the documents, which were then tested for authenticity. To their relief, when the handwriting was compared with a sample of Hitler's, the text was confirmed by three independent experts as definitely having been penned in the Fuehrer's own hand. The handwriting assessors were Max Frei-Sultzer, previously head of the forensic science department of the Zurich Police, Ordway Hilton, a specialist document assessor from South Carolina, and the third was a documents expert from the German police. Rights to publish the diaries in other countries were sold to overseas newspapers and a lucrative bandwagon began to roll. When the Sunday Times group bought the English language rights, the prominent historian Hugh Trevor-Roper, author of *The Last Days of Hitler*, was asked to vet the diaries from a historical point of view. At first, he too was convinced they were genuine, but he later became suspicious and in April 1983, he tried unsuccessfully to delay publication.

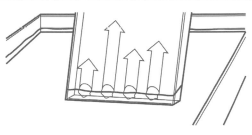

Above There are many methods used to analyze inks and documents, such as thin-layer chromotography which separates substances by the speed at which they move up a plate covered with silica gel.

The Evidence

By then the German police had taken their own look at the diaries and had already decided they were forgeries. Instead of checking the handwriting, they carried out a close forensic analysis of the materials used in the diaries—the ink, the paper, and the official seals attached to documents. They found that when seen under ultraviolet light, the paper showed a whitening agent which had not been used before 1954. The threads attaching the seals to the documents contained polyester and viscose, which had not been available during the war, and none of the four types of ink used in the documents had existed during the war years. Most decisively, the evaporation of chloride from the ink as it dried showed that the diaries had been written at most a year prior to the tests.

The Outcome

Investigations showed the diaries had been created by a small-time forger named Konrad Kujau, who had not only posed as the collector who had found the diaries but had also produced some of the samples of so-called "genuine" Hitler handwriting used by the experts to authenticate the diaries! In 1985 Kujau and Heidemann were put on trial for fraud. Both were found guilty—the forger was sentenced to four and a half years in prison, while the journalist was given an additional two months.

Written in Blood

Where:	Mougins, France
When:	June 23, 1991
Culprit:	unproven
Victim:	Ghislaine Marchal
Cause of death:	stabbed and beaten to death
Forensic technique:	handwriting analysis

The Crime

Sometimes forensic evidence fails to prove a suspect committed a crime; different items of physical evidence can contradict one another and the truth becomes obscured. But in a few cases, it can at least help to avoid the wrong person being punished for a crime they did not commit. In the case of wealthy 65-year-old widow Ghislaine Marchal, stabbed and beaten to death in the cellar of her own villa in Mougins near Cannes on June 23, 1991, the clues were easy to find.

The Case

While dying from her wounds, she had written on the wall in her own blood the damning words *"Omar m'a tuer…"* or "Omar has killed me." Her gardener, a Moroccan called Omar Raddad, had disappeared, apparently taking with him 4,000 francs believed to be in the house at the time. Raddad did not remain at large for long. After being captured he was charged with Mme Marchal's murder and put on trial on January 24, 1992. His defense was that at the time she was supposed to have been murdered, he had been sent on an errand to Cannes to buy bread, but he was found guilty and sentenced to 18 years in prison, despite protesting his complete innocence of the crime.

The Evidence

Then doubts began to surface. Mme Marchal was known to be a clever, well-educated woman, addicted to crossword puzzles. Though the prosecution found a graphologist to claim that the bloody message was indeed in her writing, would she really have mistakenly used the infinitive form of the verb tuer, meaning "to kill," rendering the message almost meaningless? She would almost certainly have used the word tuée or "killed," as a matter of instinct and basic grammar, even at such a desperate moment. The defense brought in two other graphologists who claimed there were clear differences between the writing on the wall and Mme Marchal's hand, as revealed when compared with completed crossword puzzles found in her villa.

She had been found dead in the cellar, behind a door barricaded from the inside by an iron bar and an iron bedstead. Her hand was covered in blood, but detectives never checked the width of her fingertips to confirm that it was actually her who had written the message. In fact, medical experts doubted anyone so grievously wounded could have written any message at all.

Other contradictions continued to blur the picture: a pair of bloodstained gloves, found in the kitchen sink, had been burned in the fireplace, together with Mme Marchal's diary; there was no trace of blood on the clothing Raddad was wearing at the time; and DNA tests on the blood in the cellar showed it was a mixture of Mme Marchal's blood and that of an unknown male, who was definitely not Raddad. Finally, Professor Fournier, an expert in forensic medicine, was convinced that the murder had actually been carried out on the same day as the discovery of the body, a day later than claimed at the trial. If this was the case, Omar Raddad had a cast-iron alibi, having spent the day with relatives and friends in Toulon.

The Outcome

Increasing doubts, and the efforts of Raddad's defense team, finally resulted in a partial Presidential pardon in 1998. Having served four years of his sentence, Omar Raddad was released on September 4, and started work in a halal butcher's shop in Marseilles ten days later. But so far his campaign for a retrial to reverse what he insists is a miscarriage of justice has been unsuccessful. The prosecution still insist he killed his employer to steal money to pay off gambling debts, but the defense say he is merely a scapegoat for family members trying to steal from their wealthy relative.

Part Eight:

Trace Evidence
and DNA

Anatomy of Murder

Where:	Boston, Massachusetts, USA
When:	November 23, 1849
Culprit:	Dr. John Webster
Victim:	Dr. George Parkman
Cause of death:	beaten to death
Forensic technique:	odontology

The Crime

Boston's academic circles were shaken by a mysterious disappearance in the approach to the Thanksgiving holiday of November 1849. Dr. George Parkman had made the mistake of lending $438, a substantial sum of money at that time, to Dr. John Webster, professor of chemistry and mineralogy at Harvard's Medical College, and was having trouble recovering the money. On Friday November 23, he went to Webster's office and laboratory, to deliver the ultimatum that unless the money was repaid, Parkman would condemn him to social and professional ruin by making his debt public knowledge.

He never returned home. Within days his wife had published posters begging for information and promising a reward, but to no avail. Webster admitted Parkman had called at his office but claimed that the debt had been repaid in full. He suggested that Parkman may have been attacked by thieves and murdered on his way home, and there was a supposed sighting of him at around 5 PM that same afternoon on the opposite side of the city.

The Case

But Parkman was never seen alive again. His fate was revealed by a janitor at the Medical College named Ephraim Littlefield. On the day Parkman had visited Webster and then disappeared, Littlefield had found the dividing wall with Webster's locked office was extremely hot to the touch. On the other side of the wall was an assay oven used for Webster's work, and when Littlefield asked why the wall was so hot, Webster said he had been conducting experiments. He seemed shifty, which made the janitor suspicious, and when the notoriously mean and hard-up professor then offered him a Thanksgiving turkey for himself and his family, Littlefield was determined to find out the truth. When Webster left his office, Littlefield told his wife to keep watch in case he returned, and then he set about breaking through the wall into the laboratory. On discovering a human pelvis and two parts of a leg, and nothing to do with any conceivable experiments Webster could have been conducting, Littlefield called the police.

The Evidence

When the police searched the office, they found more human remains. The largest were parts of a human chest found in a storage box, and up to 150 bones and fragments of bones. Though there was nothing to positively identify the remains, a team of specialists measured them and confirmed that they belonged to a single victim, a male in his 50s who had been around 5 feet 10 inches (178 cm) tall. This was a fairly close match to the missing Parkman, who was 5 feet 11 inches (180 cm) tall and just 60 years old, but the final crucial detail was found in the ashes contained in the office oven: a set of dentures which had survived the high temperatures. They were compared with the original mold kept by Parkman's dentist, Dr. Nathan Keep, and as the result was a perfect match, the remains were assumed to be those of the missing Parkman. Webster maintained they were those of a corpse used in medical students' anatomy classes, but the absence of embalming fluid and the degree of decomposition suited the time scale since Parkman's disappearance.

The Outcome

At Webster's trial, his lawyer tried to discredit the dental evidence by producing another set of dentures unrelated to the case which also fitted Dr. Keep's mould. Webster's attempt to commit suicide by taking strychnine nevertheless suggested his guilt, and he was finally convicted and executed the summer after Parkman's disappearance. For the first time, forensic evidence had led to the conviction of a killer in the absence of a corpse with a positively proven identity. Just before he was hanged, Webster confessed to having battered Parkman to death with a wooden club and cutting up his body.

Blundering Train Robbers

Where:	Oregon, USA
When:	October 11, 1923
Culprit:	D'Autremont brothers
Victims:	Union Pacific train crew
Cause of death:	gunshot wounds
Forensic technique:	trace evidence

The Crime

When an attempt was made to rob a Union Pacific mail train in the mountains of Oregon in 1923, it seemed at first that although the criminals responsible had panicked and fled after shooting the train crew dead and blowing up the mail coach, but before seizing any of the loot, they had at least been careful to leave nothing which could lead to their identification. Detectives searching the scene of the crime found only a pair of shoe covers that had been soaked in creosote in an attempt to blot out their scent from police tracker dogs, a battery and detonator used to set off the explosives, a revolver, and a single pair of overalls. There was nothing, it would seem, to indicate who had carried out the attack.

The Case

The criminals could hardly have been more wrong. Edward Heinrich, in charge of the forensic science laboratory at Berkeley in California, subjected the overalls to a detailed examination, and came up with an astonishing amount of information on the person who had worn them. Traces of grease had been found on the material, leading police to suspect they had belonged to a garage mechanic, but Heinrich analyzed the substance in detail and revealed it came from pine trees. Small chips of Douglas fir were also found on the overalls, together with a hair stuck to one of the buttons, strands of tobacco and nail clippings, and a tiny piece of folded paper almost destroyed by having been washed while in a pocket of the overalls.

The Evidence

To the skilled investigator, this evidence resulted in the identification of the anonymous owner of the overalls: the hair found on the button of the overalls showed he was a fair-haired man in his 20s, while the size of the overalls suggested he was some 5 feet 10 inches (178 cm) tall and weighed between 154 and 168 pounds (70 and 76 kg). The tree grease and chippings suggested he worked as a lumberjack, the tobacco revealed he rolled his own cigarettes, and the nail clippings that he was unusually careful about his appearance for someone working as a tree feller. He was identified as being left-handed by the differences in wear patterns on the overalls which showed he buttoned them from the left, while the pockets on the left-hand side showed greater wear than those on the right.

But the clinching piece of evidence was the tightly rolled up, matted piece of paper. It was carefully unwrapped and treated with iodine to bring up the original printing, whereupon it proved to be evidential gold dust. It was a receipt from the US Post Office for a registered package for one Roy D'Autremont, living in Eugene, Oregon in the heart of the heavily forested region of the Northwest. Police then checked the address and spoke to neighbors who confirmed Roy matched all the descriptions produced by the forensic laboratory, but that he had disappeared, along with his brothers Ray and Hugh.

The Outcome

The police drew up descriptions of the other two brothers, and all three were posted as wanted men. At first it seemed the trail had died out, but four years after the robbery, a US Army sergeant serving in the Philippines said Hugh d'Autremont was serving in his unit. He was arrested in Manila, after which his brothers were tracked down to an Ohio steel mill, where they were working under false identities. Confronted with the evidence against them, all three confessed to the crime and were sentenced to imprisonment for life.

DNA Fingerprints

Where: Leicestershire, UK
When: September 1983 and
                 July 1986
Culprit: Colin Pitchfork
Victims: Lynda Mann and
                 Dawn Ashworth
Cause of death: strangled
Forensic technique: DNA fingerprinting

The Crime

In September 1983 and July 1986 two 15-year-old schoolgirls were raped and strangled in adjacent villages in the Leicestershire countryside. Both had been killed on secluded footpaths, so police assumed that both attacks were carried out by someone local, although they did not at first connect the two incidents. The first victim, Lynda Mann, had been killed in Narborough, while the second, Dawn Ashworth, had been visiting friends in Narborough and was returning home to Enderby. Despite exhaustive enquiries in the area and appeals for witnesses, no positive leads emerged in either case.

The Case

After the second killing, police checked computer records for local men with records of sexual offenses. One positive lead pointed to Richard Buckland, a young kitchen porter at a mental hospital on the outskirts of Narborough, and when questioned, he admitted to Dawn Ashworth's killing. But when certain errors in the details of his story made his evidence suspect, his confession was withdrawn. At this set-back in the proceedings, police contacted Dr. Alec Jeffreys in the genetics department of Leicester University, the inventor of DNA fingerprinting, to compare a sample of the suspect's DNA with evidence found on both the victims' bodies. The results were surprising. Buckland's sample matched neither of the others—but the samples from both victims were a perfect match. The same person was responsible for both killings.

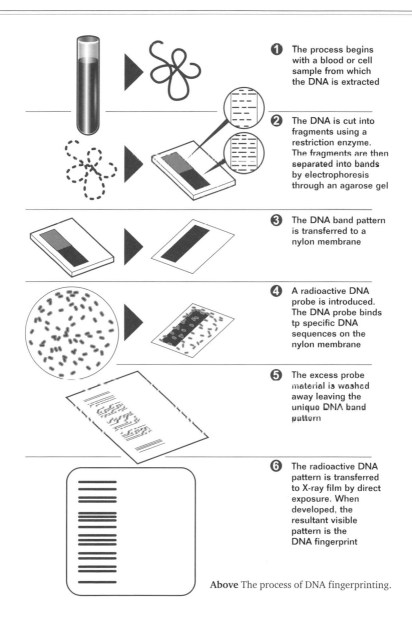

1. The process begins with a blood or cell sample from which the DNA is extracted

2. The DNA is cut into fragments using a restriction enzyme. The fragments are then separated into bands by electrophoresis through an agarose gel

3. The DNA band pattern is transferred to a nylon membrane

4. A radioactive DNA probe is introduced. The DNA probe binds tp specific DNA sequences on the nylon membrane

5. The excess probe material is washed away leaving the unique DNA band pattern

6. The radioactive DNA pattern is transferred to X-ray film by direct exposure. When developed, the resultant visible pattern is the DNA fingerprint

Above The process of DNA fingerprinting.

The Evidence

DNA analysis could now provide positive evidence of whether or not a suspect could be connected with the samples found at a crime scene, but this depended on investigators having DNA samples from the wider population to carry out comparisons. This meant requesting blood samples from the entire adult male population of Narborough and Enderby, as well as neighboring Littlethorpe as a first step. This was a huge task, involving more than 4,000 men between the ages of 16 and 34, and the cumbersome DNA comparison procedure then in use built up a large backlog. In any case, police knew the killer would try to avoid the test, but hoped that covering the entire male population in the area would eventually reveal who he was.

Then came a breakthrough that short-circuited their slow progress, and ended concerns over widening the search, an ever more daunting task, if a positive match was not identified. On August 1, 1987, four workers from a Leicester bakery were drinking in the Clarendon public house when one of them overheard a man named Ian Kelly admit he had been offered £200 by another fellow worker, Colin Pitchfork, to provide a blood sample on his behalf. The reason, according to Kelly, was that Pitchfork had once been convicted of indecent exposure, and police now gave him a rough time when under interrogation. Initially he refused, but Pitchfork then explained he had done the same thing for another friend with an indecent exposure conviction and if he was found to have given two samples under different names in a murder enquiry he would be in really serious trouble. Kelly had agreed, and Pitchfork had provided him with a modified passport as proof of identity.

The Outcome

The woman who overheard this story knew Pitchfork as a persistent sexual pest, but was reluctant at first to incriminate him and Kelly. Finally, she told police seven weeks later, and they checked their records. Pitchfork had actually been questioned in the original door-to-door enquiries, but the genuine signature on his statement did not match the signature given by Kelly with the blood sample. Pitchfork was arrested and his blood sample showed he was indeed the double murderer. He later made a full confession, and on January 22, 1988 was sentenced to life imprisonment.

Trapped by Trace Evidence

Where: Bondi, Sydney, Australia
When: July 7, 1960
Culprit: Stephen Bradley
Victim: Graeme Thorne
Cause of death: strangled and beaten to death
Forensic technique: trace evidence

The Crime

In the 1960 Sydney Opera House lottery, Bazil and Frieda Thorne bought ticket 3932, which won them a prize of 100,000 Australian pounds. Thorne was a successful traveling salesman and the family had managed to send their eight-year-old son Graeme to the highly regarded independent school, Scots College. Each weekday morning he would walk from the family home in the Sydney suburb of Bondi to pick up a lift from the mother of two of his schoolmates in the next road. But on Thursday July 7 he disappeared. The family's sudden and well-publicized new wealth had made him the victim of the first child kidnapping for ransom in Australia's history.

The Case

The Thornes reported their son's disappearance, and police sergeant Larry O'Shea was in the house when the kidnapper rang, demanding 25,000 Australian pounds by five o'clock that day or the boy would be killed. The man spoke with a thick East-European accent, and said he would call back later with orders on how the ransom was to be paid. The second call never came, but a massive media campaign helped to produce pieces of evidence. Graeme's school case, cap, lunch box, coat, and math books were found scattered along a busy highway leading to the seaside town of Seaforth. But the boy himself was not found until August 16, when children found a bundle hidden under a rock ledge on a Seaforth vacant site. It contained the eight-year-old's body, still dressed in school clothes and wrapped in a traveling rug. He had been bound hand and foot, and strangled and beaten to death.

The Evidence

In the meantime, neighbors had told investigators that they had seen a blue 1955 model Ford Customline on the morning of the abduction, close to where Graeme had vanished. Police had embarked on the huge task of checking owners of every car matching the description when coverage of the discovery of the body brought a call from William and Kathleen Telford, who lived in Clontarf, the next suburb to Seaforth. They told police that their neighbor, Steven Bradley, had this type and color of car but he seemed to have gone away. They said he had been born Hungarian and had a pronounced accent. The police questioned Bradley at work, but he denied all knowledge of the abduction. They released him while they searched for more evidence, only to find that he, along with his wife and three children, had left for England on the passenger liner *Himalaya*, and his car had vanished altogether.

More evidence was uncovered from Graeme's body. There were traces of mold on his shoes and socks, cypress seeds and animal hairs on his clothing, and some unusual pink grains. The development of the mold at the time the body was found showed that he must have died at about the time he was kidnapped, while the animal hairs were found to belong to a Pekinese dog. The pink grains were from an unusual type of mortar used in house construction and the cypress seeds were from a variety that was not found where the body had been left.

The Bradleys' house, however, matched all the abundant evidence. It had pink mortar between the bricks, the right type of cypress in the garden, as well as a photograph showing a family picnic on the very rug used to wrap Graeme's body. The missing car was finally tracked down to a used car dealership, where a search revealed traces of pink mortar in the boot, and the Bradleys' missing Pekinese dog was found in a veterinary hospital.

The Outcome

Australian police were sent to Sri Lanka, where the *Himalaya* was due to pause on its voyage. After convincing the initially skeptical Sri Lankan authorities of the strength of their case, they brought the family back to Australia. Stephen Bradley was tried for the murder of Graeme Thorne, convicted, and sentenced to life imprisonment.

The Fox

Where:	Southern England, UK
When:	April–August 1984
Culprit:	Malcolm Fairley
Victims:	numerous
Crime:	theft and rape
Forensic technique:	paint analysis

The Crime

Criminals who evade detection for their crimes often become more ambitious and even more violent. One serial burglar, who had been breaking into houses in Buckinghamshire, Bedfordshire, and Hertfordshire to the north of London between April and August 1984 found a shotgun at the scene of one of his crimes, which he subsequently used to terrorize his victims. If he found a house empty, he would wait for the occupants to return before assaulting the males and attempting to rape any females. His cunning and violence led to him being nicknamed "The Fox."

The Case

To prevent victims identifying him, he wore a hooded mask cut from the legs of a pair of overalls. Those who suffered at his hands helped police to build up a profile. Slim and soft-spoken, with long fingers, he was left-handed and thought to come from north-east England. But catching him proved impossible until August 19, when he set out to visit his mother in County Durham. On the way, he stopped at the junction of the M1 and M18 motorways, intending to commit another attack, as he had his shotgun and disguise with him. He stopped on the hard shoulder, backed his car into a wood, and walked across the fields to a small south Yorkshire village called Brampton-en-le-Morthen. He broke into a house and found a couple asleep. He tied up the man and raped the woman, cutting away the bed sheet afterward to remove any evidence. He then returned to the car and hid the mask, gun, and a pair of gloves before resuming his journey. It proved to be a fatal mistake.

The Evidence

The Fox committed two more attacks in County Durham before returning south and resuming his burglaries around Milton Keynes. However, when details of the Brampton attack were entered on the police computer, the description of the attacker and his routine suggested that this was also the handiwork of The Fox. And this time he had made a series of errors. Police were able to trace his footprints from the house he had entered, all the way back to the spot where he had left his car. They found his mask, gloves, and gun, all barely concealed under leaves, and a set of tire marks. Then they found one more tiny but crucial detail—a heart-shaped fleck of paint that had been dislodged from the car when he reversed into the bushes. The color was identified as "Harvest Gold," a shade used only on Austin Allegros made between May 1973 and August 1975.

Armed with this evidence, police started visiting all potential criminals on their lists who had moved from the north-east to the area around London, and who were thought to drive Austin Allegros. On September 11, 1984, two officers from the investigation team were sent to check an address in Oseney Crescent in the North London suburb of Kentish Town. There they found the occupant, Malcolm Fairley, outside in the road washing his car, an Austin Allegro finished in Harvest Gold. When questioned, the officers noticed his north-eastern accent, and when they asked him to pick up his watch from the back seat of the car and put it on, he showed he was left-handed. The car showed traces of scratches at the same height as the sapling where the paint flake had been found at Brampton. It appeared The Fox had been run to earth.

The Outcome

Inside Fairley's flat, police found sets of overalls made from identical material to that his mask was made from. Faced with the mass of evidence against him, he admitted to the crimes and on February 26, 1985, less than 12 months after his series of attacks began, he was given six life sentences.

The Soham Murders

Where:	Soham, Cambridgeshire, UK
When:	August 5, 2002
Culprit:	Ian Huntley
Victims:	Holly Wells and
	Jessica Chapman
Crime:	murder
Forensic technique:	trace evidence

The Crime

In the Cambridgeshire village of Soham, two ten-year-olds, Holly Wells and
Jessica Chapman, vanished on Monday August 5, 2002. They were last seen
at 6:30 PM, walking through the village before they disappeared. The last
person to see them alive seemed to have been school caretaker Ian Huntley.
Eventually this proved all too true, as he had killed them both.

The Case

Police searched potential hiding places, including Huntley's house at 5 College
Close. Since then, Huntley and his girlfriend Maxine Carr had cleaned both
house and car very thoroughly. A cell phone expert revealed that the girls' cell
had probably been switched off outside 5 College Close and police turned
their attention to Huntley. They were still unaware of his checkered record of
violence to women and sex with underage girls, but after he was interviewed
on national television, a woman from Humberside told police he had appeared
in court there on a charge of rape. Police checked the records, and realized his
full history. Under police questioning Maxine claimed she had been upstairs
in the bath when Huntley had briefly spoken to the girls outside the house.

The Evidence

Huntley and Carr maintained their story when questioned, but in a thorough
search of the house police found a key to a storage hangar at Huntley's
workplace. In the bins inside it, they found burned items of the girls' clothing
in bin liners covered with Huntleys' fingerprints. The following morning, on

Above Burnt remains of a shoe belonging to one of the murdered girls, found hidden in a bin.

August 17, both Huntley and Carr were arrested, and later that same day the mystery of the girls' fate was tragically solved. A gamekeeper and his girlfriend, walking in the countryside near RAF Lakenheath some miles north-east of Soham, noticed an appalling smell of rotting flesh. When they looked for the source, they found the two small bodies dumped in a waterlogged ditch.

Police found Huntley's hairs on the clothing fragments in the bins. Though the car tires and boot lining had been changed, they found ten red fibers from the girls' Manchester United shirts inside the vehicle. In all they found 154 fibers from the girls' clothing inside the house. Finally, they found mud and pollen grains on the car's underside which perfectly matched conditions at the site where their bodies had been left. Faced with increasing forensic evidence, Huntley finally changed his story.

The Outcome

He admitted that the girls had come to the house, asking after Maxine, when Holly suffered a nosebleed. Huntley had been washing his dog in the bathroom and had tried to stop the bleeding when Holly had slipped and fallen into the bath. Jessica had started screaming that he had pushed her, and to keep her quiet he had put his hand over her mouth only to find she had suffocated, by which time Holly too was dead. The jury didn't believe his version of events and found him guilty of the girls' murders. He was given two life sentences, and in September 2005 his minumum term was set at 40 years in prison.

Errors in Procedure

Where:	Los Angeles, California, USA
When:	June 12, 1994
Culprit:	unproven
Victims:	Nicole Brown-Simpson and Ronald Goldman
Cause of death:	throat wounds
Forensic technique:	serology

The Crime

O.J. Simpson was famous as both a football star and a film actor. In 1985, he married a glamorous second wife, Nicole Brown-Simpson and the couple had two children. But cracks in the relationship began to appear, and eventually his violent behavior led to a divorce in 1992. Then, on the misty Sunday evening of June 12, 1994, neighbors living close to Nicole's home at 875 South Bundy Drive in the Los Angeles suburb of Brentwood, were disturbed by the agitated barking of her dog. When they tried to calm it down they saw its paws were soaked in blood. Approaching the house they could clearly see a body lying inside the gate, and immediately called police to the scene.

The Case

The body was that of Nicole, and close by was the body of her friend Ronald Goldman. Both had bled to death after horrific throat wounds. Police tried to contact Simpson, who lived five minutes' drive away, but he had left earlier that evening on a trip to Chicago. On his return he was at first questioned informally by the police, but as more and more evidence started to point to him as the killer, police issued an arrest warrant on June 17. Simpson and his lawyer failed to report as ordered, but Simpson was spotted driving his Ford Bronco, accompanied by close friend Al Cowling, who warned police that their suspect was suicidal. A bizarre chase ensued, shown on TV, with police pursuing the runaway vehicle at 40 mph (65 kph), followed by helicopters, until the fugitive finally drove back to his home and submitted to arrest.

The Evidence

On the face of it, the evidence against Simpson was damning. Numerous people had heard him threaten his ex-wife, and he had broken into her previous home and attacked her. DNA profiling of the blood at the crime scene showed the presence of a third person's blood, later matched to that of Simpson. There

Above Simpson puts on one of the bloody gloves during his trial; one was found at the scene, the other at his house.

were also bloodstained footprints from a size 12 Bruno Magli shoe, a design known to have been worn by him. At his initial interview, police noticed that his left hand was cut—a bloody left-hand glove was found beside the bodies, the right-hand glove was outside Simpson's home. Finally, drops of the victims' blood were found in Simpson's Ford Bronco, and at his home.

The Outcome

It was difficult to find a more watertight mass of evidence, yet in the end Simpson was acquitted. His energetic 11-lawyer defense team attacked every conclusion of the forensic team, and insisted the actions of the investigators were governed by racism and personal malice. For example, Simpson said he had never owned a pair of Bruno Magli shoes, even though press photographs clearly showed him wearing them, and when he was asked to try on the gloves in court, his lawyer insisted he try them on over a pair of latex gloves, so unsurprisingly they were too small. The trial lasted for nine months, but in the end the jury was divided along racial lines and the crime remains unsolved, a powerful example to underline that even first-class forensic evidence can be rendered useless by small errors in procedures and collecting samples. Significantly, the victims' families later brought a civil prosecution against Simpson, in which he was found guilty and ordered to pay punitive damages.

Cracking an Alibi

Where:	Orlando, Florida, USA
When:	May 1986–March 1987
Culprit:	Tommy Lee Andrews
Victims:	numerous young women
Crime:	rape
Forensic technique:	DNA evidence

The Crime

When criminals repeatedly commit crimes without being caught, sometimes they become more adept at the routine of their crimes, for example at breaking into a house or concealing evidence that may identify and incriminate them. Sometimes, though, they become careless, and their growing experience will be offset by either a trivial mistake or a new advance in the capabilities of forensic science. A violent series of rapes in Orlando, Florida began on May 9, 1986, when a 27-year-old female computer operator was surprised by an intruder in her flat. He threatened her with a knife and raped her three times before stealing her bag and vanishing. He had kept her face covered during the attack, but was unaware she had caught a glimpse of him when he first surprised her. He went on to commit a long series of rapes and thefts, 23 in total over a period of seven months, always taking care to cover the faces of his victims to prevent them identifying him. Then he made his second mistake, when he left a clear set of fingerprints around a window when he entered a victim's home and raped her while her children were asleep in the next-door bedroom.

The Case

Unfortunately, the rapist's fingerprints did not match any in police records. However, on March 1, 1987, police were led to the scene of a reported prowler, and arrived in time to spot a blue Ford racing away from the area at high speed. They had followed it for two miles when the driver misjudged a bend and crashed. He was arrested and identified as Tommy Lee Andrews, and his fingerprints were found to match those left at the earlier attack.

Furthermore, his first victim, Nancy Hodge, who had glimpsed his face briefly, had no hesitation in identifying him as her attacker. The chances of a conviction were good, but only if he was convicted of both attacks would he be sent away for a long jail term. If he was found guilty of only one, he might only be imprisoned for a medium-term sentence, but police were convinced they had caught the man responsible for many more vicious attacks—was there nothing which would prove he had carried out both rapes, and qualify for life imprisonment?

The Evidence

The answer was, yes—the same DNA fingerprinting technique that had been used to convict Colin Pitchfork of the rape and murder of two schoolgirls in England. In what became the first case in the United States where DNA evidence was crucial in convicting a criminal, samples of Andrews' blood and semen were checked against samples preserved from Nancy Hodge, and the result was a perfect match. However, Andrews was given an apparently unshakeable alibi by his girlfriend and sister, and the DNA comparison technique was so new and complex that the prosecution were tripped up during cross-examination. The jury divided, with one member of the 12 not accepting Andrews' guilt, and the result was declared a mistrial. On the charge of raping the other victim where fingerprints had been found at the scene, he was found guilty as charged and sentenced to 22 years in prison.

The Outcome

That was not the end of the story though. In February 1988 he was tried again for the Nancy Hodge rape and the battle lines were drawn once more. His sister and girlfriend repeated their evidence that he had been with them at the time, while his victim repeated her positive identification. The big difference on this occasion was that the DNA case was absolutely watertight, and the jury agreed unanimously that he had been responsible for raping this young woman too. The sentence amounted to a total of 115 years.

Glossary

Alpha radiation: highly toxic stream of alpha particles emitted from radioactive substances like polonium-210.

Antigens: chemical molecules which attach themselves to the basic red blood cells to create the different blood groups.

Ballistics: the study of firearms and the bullets and pellets they discharge.

Cricoid cartilage: ring-shaped cartilage in the larynx, often damaged in cases of strangulation.

DNA: deoxyribonucleic acid, the molecules of which provide the genetic blueprint for the living creature which carries it, and in the case of human beings a unique identifier of each individual.

Forensic anthropologist: specialist in skeletal remains, who can determine whether or not they are human, and reveal details of stature, gender, age, and occupational damage.

Forensic chemist: specialist in chemical analyses, including drugs and samples of dyes and paints found at a crime scene.

Forensic entomologist: specialist in the different types and forms of insects found on a corpse, which can reveal details such as the time of death.

Forensic serologist: specialist in the study of bodily substances, including blood and DNA.

Gallstone: hard chemical deposits found in the gall bladder and bile ducts, which are resistant to acids and which often have to be removed surgically.

Gastric juices: the highly acidic chemicals generated within the human stomach to break down food as the first stage of the digestive process.

Hemoglobin: the blood protein which transports oxygen from the lungs to the body tissues.

Hypocalcination: an abnormal dental condition which relates to calcium deficiency, producing deep pits in the upper surfaces of teeth that cause an unusual bite mark.

Latent fingerprints: fingerprints invisible to the naked eye, but which can be revealed by a range of different specialist chemicals and techniques.

Nucleotides: basic units which make up the DNA double helix chain, each one consisting of one of four types of base linked to a sugar phosphate molecule.

Proteins: organic compounds which play a vital part in the structure and function of all living cells.

Red corpuscles: disk-like cells in the bloodstream which carry the hemoglobin which transports oxygen to body tissues.

Ricin: highly toxic protein isolated from the castor bean which causes red blood cells to clump together, interfering with oxygen supplies to vital organs.

Rifling: spiral grooves cut in the inner surface of a gun barrel which make the bullet spin when fired, to improve its accuracy, but which also give it a unique identity which can be revealed under a microscope.

Striations: fine marks in the rifling grooves of a gun barrel caused by the cutting tool in its manufacture, which add to the individual marks on any bullet fired from the weapon.

Toxicology: the specialist study of poisons, their effects on the human body, and the tests which can reveal their presence in victims.

Voiceprint: a graphical trace of the amplitudes and frequencies of the sound of a person speaking a given word.

Sources

Evans, Colin, *The Casebook of Forensic Detection*, (John Wiley & Sons: New York, 1996).

Knight, Bernard, *Simpson's Forensic Medicine*, (Arnold: London, 1996)

Kurland, Michael, *How to Solve a Murder: The Forensic Handbook*, (Macmillan: New York, 1995).

Lane, Brian, *The Encyclopedia of Forensic Science*, (Headline Book Publishing: London, 1992)

Nickell, Joe, Detecting *Forgery: the Forensic Examination of Documents*, (University of Kentucky Press, 1996).

Owen, David, *Air Accident Investigation, 3rd edition*, (Patrick Stevens Limited: Yeovil, 2006).

Owen, David, *Hidden Evidence*, (Time Life Books: London, 2000).

Owen, David, *Criminal Minds, The Science and Psychology of Profiling*, (Barnes and Noble: New York, 2004)

Saferstein, Richard, *Criminalistics*, (Prentice Hall: New York, various editions).

Wambaugh, Joseph, *The Blooding*, (Bantam Books: New York, 1989).

Wecht, Dr Cyril (intro), *Crime Scene Investigation*, (Readers Digest: New York, Montreal, 2004).

Zonderman, Jon, *Beyond the Crime Lab, The New Science of Investigation*, (John Wiley & Sons: New York, 1990).

Index

Index

HarperCollins books may be purchased for educational,
business, or sales promotional use. For information, please
write: Special Markets Department, HarperCollins
Publishers, 10 East 53rd Street, New York, NY 10022.

FIRST U.S. EDITION

ISBN-13: 978-0-06-137420-3

Conceived and produced by
Elwin Street Limited
144 Liverpool Road
London N1 1LA
www.elwinstreet.com

Design: James Lawrence
Illustrations: Richard Burgess
Picture Credits: Corbis: p. 99;
Getty Images: pp. 45, 49, 90, 95, 131, 136;
Science Photo Library: pp. 32, 115;
Topfoto: pp. 66, 73, 75, 106

Printed and bound in China